CASCADE
COMPANION
TO EVIL

CASCADE COMPANIONS

The Christian theological tradition provides an embarrassment of riches: from Scripture to modern scholarship, we are blessed with a vast and complex theological inheritance. And yet this feast of traditional riches is too frequently inaccessible to the general reader.

The Cascade Companions series addresses the challenge by publishing books that combine academic rigor with broad appeal and readability. They aim to introduce nonspecialist readers to that vital storehouse of authors, documents, themes, histories, arguments, and movements that comprise this heritage with brief yet compelling volumes.

RECENT TITLES IN THIS SERIES:

CASCADE COMPANION TO EVIL

CHARLES TALIAFERRO

 CASCADE *Books* · Eugene, Oregon

CASCADE COMPANION TO EVIL

Cascade Companions

Cascade Books
An Imprint of Wipf and Stock Publishers
199 W. 8th Ave., Suite 3
Eugene, OR 97401

www.wipfandstock.com

PAPERBACK ISBN: 978-1-7252-8820-1
HARDCOVER ISBN: 978-1-7252-8818-8
EBOOK ISBN: 978-1-7252-8821-8

Cataloguing-in-Publication data:

Names: Taliaferro, Charles, author.

Title: Cascade companion to evil / Charles Taliaferro.

Description: Eugene, OR : Cascade Books, 2020 | Series: Cascade Companions | Includes bibliographical references.

Identifiers: ISBN 978-1-7252-8820-1 (paperback) | ISBN 978-1-7252-8818-8 (hardcover) | ISBN 978-1-7252-8821-8 (ebook)

Subjects: LCSH: Good and evil. | Good and evil—Religious aspects. | Theodicy.

Classification: LCC E185.9.M6 T35 2020 (print) | LCC BJ1401 (ebook)

Manufactured in the U.S.A.   11/06/20

For Peggy and Champe Taliaferro
Kris and Jim Ulland

CONTENTS

ACKNOWLEDGMENTS

I THANK ROBIN PARRY, editor for Cascade Books and Pick-wick Publishers, for inviting me to write the *Cascade Companion to Evil*. I am very grateful for the editorial assistance of Alyssa Medin and to Robin Attfield for his wise advice. I thank my wife, the great American painter and writer Jil Evans, for her inspiring grace and creativity (www.jilevans-site.com). I thank Barclay Marcell, my sister, for her brilliant, enriching, weekly spiritual blog, Shadows and Shelter (www.shadowsandshelters.com). I also acknowledge Jim Polk, my brother, for his supportive wit and wisdom.

> "How good and pleasant it is, when brothers live together in unity! It is like fine oil upon the head that runs down the head that runs down upon the beard." (Psalm 133:1–2)

I dedicate this book to Peggy and Champe Taliaferro, whose love inspired my nephew Jonathan Wells to foster family gatherings long after the passing of my parents. *Let light perpetual shine upon them*. This is also dedicated to Kris and Jim Ulland, who shed the light of healing and life-affirming friendship on those around them.

INTRODUCTION

DESPITE ONE INTERPRETATION OF its title, *The Cascade Companion to Evil* is not a friendly guide to doing evil, though it could be used for that purpose. The term "companion" comes from the Latin words *com* for "with" and *panis* for "bread," or *one who shares bread with another*— suggesting friendliness or closeness. However, I have written this guide for those who are chiefly friends of what the Christian tradition refers to as *the good, the true, and the beautiful*, rather than for those devoted to doing evil.

One reason why this book on evil will give some primacy to the good is that it grapples with the question of the role of goodness over evil and whether evil is dependent upon that which is good. Goodness, like the health of a person, seems to be a good in itself; health is not merely or primarily the absence of disease. In contrast, evil acts or events are often dependent upon the presence of goodness: good persons or good things. The reason why the destruction of an innocent person is evil is that it involves the destruction of the good of an innocent person. Unless intervening circumstances arise, it is hard to see how destroying something that is of no intrinsic value or goodness might be evil. For example, it would be quite strange to claim that destroying a lifeless meteor was itself evil; we might even think it good to destroy a massive meteor if it was on a collision course with earth. Much of what we think of as evil—murder, rape, lying, racism, sexism, oppression—all seem to involve the violation of what is good, indeed what is precious or sacred: the great goodness of human life. On the contrary, the goodness of what we value, like courage, friendship, and love, is not a matter of violating something evil. Arguably, courage, friendship, and love are inimical to cowardice, hostility, and hate, yet they are positive goods or values for their own sake.

The first chapter, *Good versus Evil*, will consider further why a guide to what is evil needs to give center stage to guiding us to value what is good.

I was invited to write this book *from a Christian point of view*. This was an irresistible invitation as I had just finished co-editing with Chad Meister a six-volume *History of Evil* covering all religious and secular approaches to evil with over 130 scholars from around the globe.[1] I enthusiastically recommend the multi-volume work addressing evil from the standpoint of Hinduism, Islam, and many other traditions, including secular naturalism. The series on evil, involving eight years of research, editing, and writing, was a monumental task in cross-cultural, global philosophy, while this book has allowed me to write from the standpoint of my own religion, Christianity. I dearly love many non-Christian traditions, and yet however much I seek to learn from Hinduism and Buddhism (this comes across, I hope, in the recent book *Is God Invisible? An Essay on Religion and Aesthetics* co-authored with Jil Evans), I am

1. These six volumes were published in 2018 by Routledge: *Evil in Antiquity* (Vol. 1), *Evil in the Middle Ages* (Vol. 2), *Evil in the Early Modern Age* (Vol. 3), *Evil in the 18th and 19th Centuries* (Vol. 4), Evil in the early 20th Century (Vol. 5), and *Evil from the Mid-20th Century to Today* (Vol. 6).

a practicing Christian rather than being thoroughly secular or practicing another religion.[2] Even so, I have written this book for both Christian and non-Christian readers (as well as those who might be in-between). I advocate a Christian philosophy of evil that I believe should be of interest to non-Christians who are open-minded about what Christianity has to offer. For example, Christian notions of forgiveness and redemption might be welcomed by many non-Christians.

The rest of this introduction is devoted to sketching the diverse Christian traditions that are at the heart of this companion to evil. Before turning to this task, I think a single paragraph might be in order about how I came to be a Christian philosopher. I often value knowing *something* of an author's background and my tale bears on a theme in chapter 2, but if this is not your cup of tea, please skip the next paragraph. I should also add that while the next paragraph addresses my journey to Christianity as an adult, this *Companion to Evil* is intended as an introductory, scholarly guide to the topic of evil from a Christian point of view, not a case of Christian apologetics in which my primary aim is to prompt you to join me in such a journey.[3]

I grew up in a Christian household on the East Coast of the United States, shaped in large part by the faith of my

2. Taliaferro and Evans, *Is God Invisible?*

3. In general, professional philosophers take a condescending view of apologetics. They tend to think of apologists as missionaries or preachers as opposed to philosophers (a term that is derived from the Greek *philo*, meaning "love," and *sophia*, meaning "wisdom," and so "philosophy" is often characterized as "the love of wisdom"). I do not share a negative view of apologetics. Many of those who are described (sometimes self-described) as apologists seem to love wisdom and, in a sense, every time philosophers argue for a position, they can well be described as apologists. I recently contributed to a volume on apologetics that may be of interest: Forrest and McGrath, eds., *The History of Apologetics*.

mother, Margaret ("Peggy") Taliaferro; although my father, Champe, a professional pilot, had scientific reservations about religion, he was a man of faith in the last decades of his life.[4] My family background and the liturgy of the Episcopal Church was sustaining in my youth, even helping me to survive a kind of *Lord of the Flies* all-boy boarding school where, one night, some of my classmates blew up three of our teachers' cars, burned down a chapel built by Native Americans, and broke into the main chapel to drink the communion wine. I cite the latter as I was in the chapel at the time praying aloud for God's mercy, unaware of the arsonists until I heard them laughing at me. In that fall of 1967 as a fifteen-year-old, I came to think that God gives us a great deal of freedom to destroy what is precious. Despite the carnage and brutality in boarding school and the chaos of the 1960s (two of my brothers did military service in the Vietnam War), Christianity made sense to me until I came under the spell of a counter-culture with lots of psychedelic drugs (LSD, mescaline) inspired by Aldous Huxley, Timothy Leary, and the Beatles, swinging back and forth between atheism and pantheism (God is everything). I recovered from what turned out to be a chaotic, graveyard spiral (not just metaphorically) in a Christian community in England first, then Switzerland called L'Abri.[5] It was there that I encountered loving, mature persons of faith who had read the

---

4. My mother later published the Christian stories and teaching that I and my siblings grew up on: *The Real Reason for Christmas* (1982), *Do You Ever Have Questions Like These?* (1991), *Easter Happiness and You* (2000), and *In the Beginning: An Account of the Old Testament for Young People* (2004). She also wrote a biography of my father as a pilot, *A Reckless Grace: An Account of Pilots and Their Planes from the Jenny to the Jets* (2008).

5. I offer a portrait of my time at L'Abri in the book *Love. Love. Love.* The title comes from the last words my father said to me before he died; he repeated the word "love" three times.

same books as I had (Sartre and Camus), plus many more (from Plato to Marcuse) and yet came to Christian conclusions. From that time in 1972 onwards, I began my adult life as a Christian, eventually pursuing graduate education in theology and philosophy, evolving into being a college philosophy professor. I continue to practice Christianity, inspired by the seventeenth-century Cambridge Platonists, based on a blend of reasons and experience that are explored in *The Golden Cord: A Short Book on the Sacred and Secular.* The Cambridge Platonists were among the first to practice philosophy in the English language (earlier work in the West was in Greek or Latin); I inherit from them a love for philosophical acumen along with an openness to meditation and transformative, mystical experience.[6]

Back to the main task of this introduction: Most Christian philosophers over the last two thousand years understand God to be supremely or maximally good (unsurpassable in goodness); God is omniscient or all-knowing (there is nothing true that God does not know), and all-powerful or omnipotent, omnipresent (there is no place where God is not). God necessarily exists. That is, God is not contingent or in existence by chance occurrence. God is not the creation of some other being or law or force. God is eternal and everlasting; this has been understood either as God being timeless or outside of time (atemporal) or as God being temporal (there *is* a past, present, and future for God) while God is without a temporal beginning or end.[7] Classical Judaism and Islam largely agree with these

6. See *The Golden Cord.* For further background on Cambridge Platonism see my *Evidence and Faith* and *Cambridge Platonist Spirituality.*

7. For an admirable treatment of the coherence of these divine attributes, see Swinburne, *The Coherence of Theism.* For a less technical, great overview see Ward, *God: A Guide for the Perplexed.*

affirmations about God, but Christianity goes further in terms of the Trinity and the incarnation. The view of many Christian philosophers is that the nature of God is not homogenous, but it consists of three persons: Father, Son, and Holy Spirit, linked in mutual love and harmony. Creation is the external, outpouring of love that originates in the inner love in the Godhead. The incarnation involves the second person of the Trinity entering our world as Jesus of Nazareth. Christians affirm that atonement (at-onement) with God is made possible by the birth, teaching, healing, passion, death, and resurrection of Jesus Christ. This is a topic in chapter 2 and onward.

Many Christian philosophers recognize these tenets while also holding that God transcends our ordinary human concepts and language. That is, our language and thought allows us a glimpse into the divine nature but not to define God as one would classify terrestrial objects.

Most Christians treat the Bible (Old and New Testament) as either itself a revelation of God or as a record of God's revelation. So, Martin Luther treated the Bible as the Word of God, but many Roman Catholic theologians think of the Bible as a record of God's revelation. In the latter case, the person Jesus Christ may be seen as God's revelation as mediated by the Bible. In this view, the Bible *becomes* the Word of the Lord when it mediates or makes present the person Jesus Christ. The Bible is that through which (in Latin, *objectum quo*) God can be experienced.

The above sketch of traditional Christianity need not be understood as some kind of checklist of beliefs. Rather, the above beliefs are part of a Christian form of life involving prayer and meditation, liturgy, social service involving care for the poor and dispossessed, the founding and running of hospitals, monasteries, the building of churches, the creation of art, and so on. It also needs to be appreciated when the ideals of Christianity (the profoundly non-violent message of Jesus's Sermon on the Mount, Matthew 5–7) are in radical conflict with the injustice, racism, anti-Semitism, and oppression that has been done historically and today in the name of Christianity.

Unfortunately, in the late twentieth and early twenty-first century, Christianity is often caricatured in popular culture. Christianity has been charged with promoting an anthropomorphic, patriarchal, tribal, racist, warrior God who wields power like a capricious, abusive parent. In reply, it needs to be granted that the Christian Bible includes passages in which God seems far less than supremely good— changing His mind (actually repenting from sending a world-wide flood, Genesis 6:6), being wrathful (Romans 1:18), commanding the death of inhabitants of the land God gives to the children of Israel (Numbers 21:2–3; Deuteronomy 20:17; Joshua 6:17, 21); God is jealous (Exodus 34:14) and commands the death penalty for homosexuality (Leviticus 20:13). And in the New Testament, Jesus appears to believe that some persons deserve eschatological judgment (Luke 16; Matthew 25), even though the exact nature of that judgment is debated by New Testament scholars

I suggest that while the Bible can be cherry-picked for verses supporting a horrifying portrait of God, the Bible needs not to be seen as a unified, fixed, single source for the Christian understanding of God. Even highly conservative Christians who believe the Bible is inerrant maintain that the Bible records the way God *appeared to people*, which is not the same thing as claiming that the Bible records precisely what is actually the case. For instance, one need not interpret the passage in Joshua (10:12) that the sun literally stayed still (or the earth rotation stopped) but that *the sun appeared to the people to be stationary*.[8] In any case, over

8. As an aside, John Walton has argued that the passage has been

the first two millennia, most Christian philosophers have held that the Bible requires careful interpretation in light of Christian experience, reason, science, and the love of God and neighbor. One of the most influential philosophical theologians of all time, Saint Augustine of Hippo, held that any sound interpretation of the Bible must lead to building up the love of God and neighbor: "So anyone who thinks he has understood the divine scriptures or any part of them, but cannot by his understanding build up this double love of God and neighbor, has not yet succeeded in understanding them."[9] Augustine held that the sound interpretations of the Bible need to build up love through loving wisdom. Loveless interpretations of scripture are to be avoided.

To go back to the biblical passages cited earlier, it is on Augustinian grounds that many Christians understand the flood narrative as a teaching about God's merciful tolerance of evildoers for the sake of redemption, as addressed in chapter 2. References to God's wrath are interpreted as a passionate commitment to justice, which is something we should emulate. The so-called genocidal commands have come to be read by many as human interpolations (reflecting hyperbolic language of the Middle East and not divinely revealed precepts) and to be read today as parables.[10] References to divine jealousy can be interpreted as life-affirming.[11] Some Christians argue that the biblical pro-

misunderstood by people not aware of ancient Near Eastern omens. He argues that the language describes a particular astral positioning of the sun and moon that would indicate a dire omen to the Amorites, weakening their resolve. He presents a brief summary of his position here: https://biologos.org/articles/biblical-credibility-and-joshua-10-what-does-the-text-really-claim.

9. Augustine, *On Christian Doctrine* 1.36.40.

10. See Copan, *Is God a Moral Monster?*; Copan *Did God Really Command Genocide?*; and Ward, *Is Religion Dangerous?*

11. Or so I argue in "The Jealousy of God." See also my article

hibitions of homosexuality are either culturally bound or not applicable to mature, faithful single-sex couples, which some churches today recognize as equal in standing before God as heterosexual married couples.[12] The topic of heaven and hell will be addressed in chapters 2 and 3. Over the last two thousand years, Christians have acquired different views of hell and heaven, and some believe that Jesus makes salvation universally accessible—open to all, and not just those who in this life come to Christian faith.

The above points about how to interpret the Bible are not simple matters that can be settled easily, but it is important at the outset to realize that the Christian idea of God's goodness does not stand or fall on simple references to the Bible. The Christian philosopher Stephen Davis offers this overview:

> There are places in the Bible where many Christians find it difficult to hear God's voice. The Bible is a human as well as a divine product—there are peaks and valleys, highs and lows. What is needed especially in the light of the murkier nooks and crannies of the Bible (among which I would include the command to slaughter all the Canaanites [e.g. Deuteronomy 2:31–35] as well as the conclusion of Psalm 1:37), is what I call *theological exegesis*. This is exegesis in the light of the rule of faith. Any given text must be interpreted in the light of the Christian community's vision of the witness of the entirety of scripture.

"The Vanity of God," which argues that the good of worshipping God is *not* a matter of divine vanity.

12. The classic book that argues for the compatibility of homosexuality and Christianity is John Boswell's *Christianity, Tolerance and Homosexuality*. See also Gareth Moore, *A Question of Truth: Christianity and Homosexuality*.

> We must always view such a vision as fallible
> and amendable by further insight.[13]

It is important to take seriously this nuanced reading of the Bible, lest this companion to evil from a Christian point of view gets entrenched in the occasional vexed passage, such as the one I am glad my parents did not act on about stoning to death disobedient sons (Deuteronomy 21:18–21).

The belief that God is overwhelmingly good creates what is traditionally called *the problem of evil*. If at the heart of all reality, there is unsurpassable goodness, why is there so much evil? This book will address that question, but for now, in this introduction, let us briefly entertain this question: *is it good for there to be a problem of evil?* I suggest that it may be good that evil is a problem, not just personally but philosophically. On certain views of naturalism (there is no God, but only nature), evil is deemed natural; it is not an aberration, as the cosmos is the result of chance and necessity, without any purpose. Richard Dawkins summarizes secular naturalism succinctly: "There is, at bottom, no design, no purpose, no evil and no good, nothing but blind pitiless indifference."[14] For some determinists who claim that everything is fixed by the laws of nature, every single evil, from rape and murder to lying and betrayal, is built into the very nature of the cosmos. It is the claim of Christianity that this is not so. Evil acts and events are an aberration, a corruption or abomination, a violation of God's will and nature. Evil should not be normalized or excused. From this point of view, it would be misleading for a critic to ask this question of Christians: how can you justify there being evil? *From the Christian point of view, evil is not*

13. Davis, "The Gospels Are Reliable as Historical Factual Accounts," 426.

14. Dawkins, *River Out of Eden*, 132–33.

justified. It should not occur. This notion is embedded in the view that, at least for us humans, evil is regarded as a choice: "Today I am giving you a choice of two ways. And I ask heaven and earth to be witnesses of your choice. You can choose life or death. The first choice will bring a blessing. The other choice will bring a curse. So choose life!" (Deuteronomy 30:15).

The Bible does hint at predestination (Ephesians 1:4–5) and there have been seminal Christians who stress meticulous providence where God controls *every* detail of all reality, but many, perhaps most Christians affirm that any divine providence must include recognizing human freedom and God's granting some independence to the created order.[15] The thesis that the cosmos is sustained by God at every moment of its existence (it would cease to be if God withdrew God's sustaining power) is not the same as the thesis that God is the sole author or agent at work in the cosmos. God's sustaining a free creature involves God conserving in being a creature who can freely choose their own course of action.

So, the approach to the problem of evil from a Christian point of view is not whether doing evil is justified; it is not justified nor favored by God. And one reason why it may be good that evil is a problem within the context of Christianity is that, if Christianity is true, there is a supremely good, all powerful being who can redeem those who suffer (a theme in chapter 2).

While questioning whether evil is justified is not (or so I suggest) a good question, a different question can be asked: *if God is so powerful and good, why does God not destroy (or prevent) all evil?* That question is addressed in this book, but it is vital to realize that it is different from

15. See van Inwagen's "The Place of Chance in a World Sustained by God."

questioning why Christians think murder and other evil acts are justified or good.

On what follows: chapter 1 and 2 focus on evil and good that involves human agency. Chapter 3 addresses what may be considered natural evils—disasters such as earthquakes, floods, famines, tsunamis, animal suffering, and so on—which do not depend on human agency. Following the series format, each chapter ends with a section titled "Questions for Discussion." These include questions that are intended to stimulate your own thinking and writing. As an author and professor, I welcome feedback from readers on those questions and others you might have.

1

GOOD VERSUS EVIL

PRELIMINARY DISTINCTIONS

TODAY, THE TERMS "GOOD" and "evil" may be used with little thought of cosmic questions, let alone questions involving God. "Good" might simply mean what the speaker desires: your saying "strawberries are good" might just mean that you enjoy strawberries. In English, the term "evil" is often reserved for things or events that are outrageously bad: the holocaust is evil, but being rude to a neighbor may simply be bad. Christian tradition has sometimes distinguished between acts that are simply bad versus catastrophic acts; Roman Catholics, for example, distinguish between venial sins and mortal sins (the first kind of sin may be a fault, like being short-tempered, while the latter can be soul-destroying, like having a tendency towards extreme, out of control rage). For the most part, Christians treat all vices and wrongdoing as sin; a state of character or action is sinful when it is contrary to God's nature and will, for example breaking one of the ten commandments. Christians (as well as observant Jews and Muslims) treat evil as wrong, as something that should not occur, but also as a transgression or violation of God's will and nature.

An important element in the Christian idea of sin and evil is the teaching that we are made in the image of God (Genesis 1:27). This has been understood variously through history, but it is basically the notion that we reflect (or can reflect) in some small, vastly minute way, some aspects of the divine nature. While God has limitless power and knowledge, we may have *some* power and knowledge; while God loves, we may love; while God creates, reasons, and is purposive, we may be creative, exercise reason, and act purposively. As image-bearers of the divine, what we do and how we live can either involve homage to the divine or sacrilege. Thus, murdering an innocent human being is wrong because their life is valuable, but it is also wrong because it involves the sinful destruction of an image-bearer of God and the one committing the murder is also desecrating his or her own standing as an image-bearer of God.

Christian theology understands proximity or harmony with the divine as not just a matter of believing that there is a God or accepting any of the various precepts of the faith, but in terms of one's way of life. One might be a believing theist but a practical atheist, insofar as one's Christian theistic belief is not lived out. Conversely, someone may be an atheist and yet live a life of compassion and the pursuit of justice that is far more in keeping with God's will and nature than the lives of some so-called "believers."

DIVINE COMMANDS

There is a philosophical question that goes back over 2,300 years: what is the authoritative power of divine commands?

In Ancient Greece, this question was raised regarding the power of gods. Is something good because the gods love it or do the gods love things because they are good? This is sometimes referred to as the Euthyphro dilemma, as it appears in Plato's dialogue, the *Euthyphro*.[1] In its two-thousand-year history, some Christians, such as John Duns Scotus, William Ockham, and Martin Luther have put great stress on God's commands. But the problem with a radical, absolute divine command theory (God can make *anything* good by commanding it) is that it risks treating values as capricious. Could a divine command make child sacrifice good?[2] Most think not. It also seems that bare commands backed by power are not able to provide a basis for ethics. If an assailant points a gun at you and demands your money, we might well say you were *obliged* to give them your money (out of prudence or self-survival) but not that you were *obligated* to do so.

Many Christians have taken the view that God's very essence or nature is good or, indeed, goodness itself. This is central to the theology of those one contemporary Christian philosopher refers to as the "A Team": Augustine, Anselm, and Aquinas. By their lights, God is such that God *cannot* do evil for its own sake. This may seem paradoxical in light of biblical passages such as "for God, everything is possible" (Matthew 19:26), but keep in mind there are also biblical passages that suggest there are things God cannot do, e.g., God cannot lie (Numbers 23:19; Titus 1:2; Hebrews 6:18). This may seem a limit on God's being all-powerful or

1. A current translation of the dilemma concerns piety: "Consider this: Is the pious being loved by the gods because it is pious, or is it pious because it is being loved by the gods?" Plato, *Euthyphro* 10a (trans. G. M. A. Grube).

2. This is a question that arises in some interpretations of Genesis 22, famously engaged by Kierkegaard in *Fear and Trembling*.

omnipotent, but many Christian philosophers (especially the "A Team") have responded that the power to do evil is not a positive, divine power, but would be a defect in the case of a God of unsurpassable, uncountable goodness. This position receives some recent support from feminists who contend that conceiving of God as sheer, unalloyed power is a reflection of a skewed male obsession with power. Dorothee Soelle makes this point:

> As a woman I have to ask why it is that human beings honor a God whose most important attribute is power, whose prime need is to subjugate, whose greatest fear is equality. . . . Why should we honor and love a being that does not transcend but only reaffirms the moral level of our present male dominated culture? Why should we honor and love this being . . . if his being is in fact no more than an outsized male?[3]

It is interesting that in biblical language that refers to God as female, there is great stress on God's loving care, and not bare powers; for example, God is a comforting mother (Isaiah 66:12–13; Hosea 11:1–4; Luke 13:34), a woman in the process of giving birth (Deuteronomy 32:18; John 3:3–7), nursing (Psalm 43:8), and a midwife (Psalm 22:9). This view that God is maximally good is sometimes called *perfect being theology*.[4] This theology is pitted against the mere love or adoration of power. The twentieth-century spiritual writer Henri Nouwen cautions Christians about the love of power:

> What makes the temptation of power so seemingly irresistible? Maybe it is that power offers an easy substitute for the hard task of love. It

3. Soelle, *The Strength of the Weak*, 97.

4. For a good overview, see Rogers, *Perfect Being Theology*.

> seems easier to control people than to love
> people. . . . We have been tempted to replace love
> with power.[5]

Here let us note a difference in the theology of divine free agency and human agency. In terms of our agency, freedom involves the power to do otherwise. So, you freely give money to the relief agency Oxfam if you give money *and could have done otherwise*. Divine freedom is similar: God creates and sustains the cosmos freely, meaning God could have done otherwise. When it comes to evil, however, the divine case is different. In our case, we may freely do good or evil, whereas, in the perfect being tradition that understands God's very essence as incorruptible goodness, God *cannot* freely torture creatures for the sake of entertainment, commit murder, and other acts anchored in evil. Perfect being theology receives some support, not just from feminists, but from the long-standing belief and practice that God is to be worshiped. Worship involves awe and homage, deep reverence, and praise. It is hard to think worship of God is good if this equates to the worship of sheer, limitless *power*. I suggest that the worship of God makes greater sense in the perfect being tradition as it involves the veneration of limitless, powerful *goodness*. I return to this thesis in a final section of this chapter.

In terms of the nature of God and commands, a large number of Christian philosophers adopt a moderate position. While raw, powerful commands, unattached to goodness, seem ethically and religiously dangerous, it is not odd to think that the commands of an essentially good God would be binding. So, Christian perfect being theologians recognize the authority of divine commands that go beyond some abstract realms of good and evil. The

5. Nouwen cited by Don Thorson in *An Exploration of Christian Theology*, 162.

God of Christianity is understood to have been revealed in covenants including communal living, establishing the Passover rite, the Eucharist, holy orders, teachings about prayer and fasting, justice and charity, and the atonement or reconciliation with God.

While historically Christian philosophers have been reluctant to recognize claims about new commandments being revealed to persons after the New Testament era, a substantial number have supported the view that the mind and love of God can be continuously experienced by persons who are receptive to God experientially.[6] I have defended the evidential integrity of reported experiences of the divine, most recently in the work co-authored with Jil Evans' *Is God Invisible? An Essay on Religion and Aesthetics*.[7] But here I note an important dimension of assessing the authenticity of religious experience in Christian tradition: in Christian

6. There are many philosophical works defending the evidential value of religious experience: Kwan, *The Rainbow of Experiences, Critical Trust, and God*; Alston, *Perceiving God*; Davis, *The Evidential Force of Religious Experience*; Evans, *Natural Signs and the Knowledge of God*; Gellman, *Experience of God and the Rationality of Religious Belief*; Gellman, *Mystical Experience of God*; Gutting, *Religious Belief and Religious Skepticism*; Yandell, *The Epistemology of Religious Experience*; Wainwright, *Mysticism*. See also Taliaferro, "In Defence of the Numinous."

7. For reports of contemporary religious experience, see the Alister Hardy Religious Experience Research Centre in Lampeter, Wales. They have archived over 6,000 accounts. David Hay, former Director of the Centre when it was in Oxford, has published an important work on such reports: *Religious Experience Today*, see chapters 5, 6, and Appendix. See also Newberg and Waldman, *How God Changes Your Brain*. Their Online Survey of Spiritual Experience between 2005–7 received 300 detailed accounts of religious experience. "At the time of the experience, 63 percent said it was more real than their normal experience of reality" (p. 74). Also see the classic work, Underhill, *Mysticism*; Harvey, *Sensing Salvation*; and Gavrilyuk and Coakley, eds., *The Spiritual Senses*.

theology, authentic experiences of the divine should lead to virtues, recognizably good events as opposed to vices and evil. This criterion for assessing whether a person is truly living experientially in the presence of God (the Latin term for being in the presence of God is *Coram Deo*) goes back to Jesus in the Gospels teaching that "By their fruits you will know them" (Matthew 7:20). An authentic encounter with the God of goodness should produce goodness. St. Teresa of Avila, a sixteenth-century Spanish mystic, highlighted this sign of authenticity when examining her own (apparent) experiences of God. She confesses that if those around her were deeply skeptical of the genuine character of her experiences of the divine, she might well dismiss her apparent experiences of God as illusory—except for the overwhelmingly good impact of these experiences on her life. I cite her at length:

> I once said to the people who were talking to me in this [skeptical] way that if they were to tell me that a person whom I knew well and had just been speaking to was not herself at all, but that I saw imagining her to be so, and that they knew this was the case, I should certainly believe them rather than my own eyes. But, I added, if that person had left some jewels with me, which I was actually holding in my hands as pledges of her great love, and if, never having had any before I were thus to find myself rich instead of poor, I could not possibly believe that this was a delusion, even if I wanted to. And I said, I could show them these jewels—for all who knew me were well aware how much my soul had changed: my confessor himself testified to this, for the difference was very great in every respect, and no fancy, but such as all could clearly see.[8]

8. Theresa of Avila, *The Life of Teresa of Jesus*, 265.

This link between reported experiences of God and virtue is widely testified to throughout Christian history.[9]

So, while some Christian philosophers have given primacy to divine commands as a basis for good and evil, more have looked to basing our concepts of good and evil on the natural order, as created by God, in addition to looking to divine commands within the context of God's good creation.

THE GOOD OF NATURE AND THE NATURE OF EVIL

Some religions, such as Zoroastrianism (possibly dating back to 2000 BCE) and Manichaeism (third century CE), depict evil as a powerful force in its own right. Gnostics (first century CE) thought of God as more powerful than evil but generally claimed that the material cosmos is itself suffused with wickedness and that salvation (liberation) is to be found in escaping the realm of matter. On the other hand, Christianity has persistently sought to recognize that the created order is itself good (Genesis 1:4, 10, 12, 18, 21). This affirmation of the goodness of creation has led many Christians to understand evil as the corruption, distortion, or perversion of what is good. Augustine writes:

> When accordingly it is inquired, whence is evil, it must first be inquired, what is evil, which is nothing else than corruption, either of the measure, or the form, or the order, that belong to nature. Nature therefore which has been corrupted, is called evil, for assuredly when incorrupt it is good; but even when corrupt, so far as

9. See Evelyn Underhill's classic work, *Mysticism*. Originally published in 1910, this book helped launch a huge interest in mysticism in the English-speaking world.

it is nature it is good, so far as it is corrupted it is evil.[10]

So, when a person tortures another, the tormentor and the victim are both still valuable, beings with a principally good nature, but the tormentor is corrupt; he is involved in abuse; he is applying his powers toward a perverse, unnatural end.

Consider this passage from Augustine's *Confessions*. He proposes that if all nature were removed from some event, there would be no evil, for there would not be anything to corrupt or be corrupted. In this view, evil winds up as a kind of parasite or deprivation of what is good:

> But if corruption take away all measure, all form, all order from corruptible things, no nature will remain. And consequently, every nature which cannot be corrupted is the highest good, as is God. But every nature that can be corrupted is also itself some good; for corruption cannot injure it, except by taking away from or diminishing that which is good. . . . No nature, therefore, as far as it is nature, is evil; but to each nature there is no evil except to be diminished in respect of good. But if by being diminished it should be consumed so that there is no good, no nature would be left.[11]

I suggest that Augustine's position has great plausibility. Most of us think that human life has great value with respect to our powers: our senses, agency, and consciousness. It is good to be able to see, hear, feel, smell, taste; it is good that we are able to move, have memory, imagination, have emotions, expectations, to dream, to make things, to

10. Augustine, *Concerning the Nature of Good* (trans. John Newman), chapter 4.

11. Cited in Bourke, *The Essential Augustine*, 50, 53.

be sexual, to reproduce, to live in community. In this view, our healthy lives are a coordination of goods.

Augustine offers the following amusing image of how the coordinated goods of balance go awry when we disrupt them by hanging upside down:

> If anyone were to hang upside down, the position of the body and arrangement of the limbs is undoubtedly perverted, because what should be on top, according to the dictates of nature, is underneath, and what nature intends to be underneath is on top. This perverted attitude disturbs the peace of the flesh, and causes distress for that reason. For all that, the breath is at peace with its body and is busily engaged for its preservation; that is why there is something to endure the pain.[12]

One of the implications of the above position is that *it is the possession of good powers that enables people to do evil.* If we lacked balance and motor control, were incontinent, had terrible vision, and could not form consistent intentions or speaking, it would be very difficult to do evil acts or form evil intentions. When you think about it, a very simple evil act like throwing a rock at a person while shouting "I hate you!" is a very complex, demanding act. Identifying a suitable rock, being able to control it in your hand (or, in very creative oral acts, being able to lodge the rock in your mouth), being able to pick out a target, throw the rock (or swivel your head and then release it in the direction of the target), and being able to utter some vile reproach or curse that others would understand, requires a great deal of skill and power. G. K. Chesterton once observed: "The word 'good' has many meanings. For example, if a man were to shoot his grandmother at a range of 500 yards I should

12. Augustine, *The City of God*, Book XIX, chapter 12.

call him a good shot, but not necessarily a good man."[13] I agree, though a follower of Augustine might add that the grandmother-assassin had to have some of the qualities that constitute the good of being a human (e.g., motility, perception, coordination) to commit the heinous act.

DO YOU HAVE TO BE GOOD TO BE EVIL?

Do you have to be good to be evil? As we have seen, Augustine would answer this question affirmatively in the sense that an evildoer must have a being that is itself good (valuable in its own right). Many of us believe that when you unjustly attack an innocent person with lethal force, you in effect lose your right to life. That is, if the only way an innocent person (or someone acting on their behalf, like a police officer or soldier) can prevent you from killing them is to kill you, they are acting in a permissible way in virtue of your right of self-defense. But, from an Augustinian point of view, this still remains a regrettable homicide, because the assailant is valuable, an image-bearer of God. From the standpoint of most Christian ethicists, killing in the right of self-defense is proper (permissible, not blameworthy), but still a grave act. Some of the reluctance of Christians to see such a killing as an unabashed praiseworthy good is because they believe in the *right to self-defense*, not necessarily *a duty to defend yourself*. That is, if you are being assailed and could kill your assailant in your defense, you are also free to not kill them but to plead with them to lay aside their weapon and to embrace the path of non-violence. We do well to remember that Christ is at the heart of Christianity; Christ endured torture and death by crucifixion with non-resistance and by admonishing his disciples to not use

13. Chesterton, "Negative and Positive Morality" in *Illustrated London News*.

weapons in his defense: "Put your weapon back in its place," Jesus tells his disciple, "For all who draw the sword will die by the sword" (Matthew 26:52).

There is one more element about whether evil is dependent on the good to consider in this opening chapter. Can persons set out to do what they themselves believe to be thoroughly evil? This would seem to call for an overwhelming response: Obviously, yes! In the New Testament, St. Paul seems to attest to this. "For I want to do what I do not do, but what I hate I do" (Romans 7:15).

But some Christian philosophers have proposed that the situation is complex and suggest that a great deal of evildoing involves self-deception. If, deep down, you thoroughly believe X is evil, you believe that it should not be done—it is wrong to do X. Moreover, if you are a Christian you believe that to do X is a sin. OK, but when you do any act whatsoever, don't you have to (on some level) approve or desire or will to do X? It has been suggested that in such cases, the evildoer must deceive himself into thinking that in this one case, it is permissible or desirable or tolerable for him to do X. Imagine cases of theft or adultery or cheating. To steal, commit adultery, cheat on taxes, don't you have to think that there is something good about the act? It would be sheer madness to do these things unless there was some supposed good to be pursued. On this view, evildoing often involves pursuing a mistaken, illusory good or pursuing something that has some good in it but it is at the wrong time or with the wrong person or in conflict with greater goods—for example, integrity and promise-keeping are more important than sexual satiation or stealing to prevent bankruptcy or cheating to get a good grade.

Back to St. Paul: what might happen when we do something evil is that we know, deep down, that it should not be done, but we deceive ourselves in the moment that it is OK—just this once. This thesis is sometimes called *the guise of the good*,[14] the thesis being that when we act we have to at least act on the grounds of what we tell ourselves is good (or acceptable or merely permissible).

Thomas Aquinas endorsed this thesis:

> [E]vil as such cannot be intended, not in any way willed or desired, sincere being desirable has the nature of good, to which evil as such is contrary. And so we see that no person does any evil except intending something that seems good to the person. For example, it seems good to the adulterer that [he should] enjoy sense pleasure, and he commits adultery for that reason. And so we conclude that evil does not have an intrinsic cause.[15]

G. E. M. Anscombe has argued that we would not be agreeable to someone acting without any goal or desire that makes sense in terms of worth. She contends that the answer "for no particular reason" is not always an acceptable answer to the question "why did you do that?": "If someone hunted out all the green books in his house and spread them out carefully on the roof, and [said they did so for no particular reason] to the question 'Why' he would be unintelligible, unless as joking or mystification."[16]

One possible exception needs to be addressed: cases of addiction. In the case of an addiction, a person might have a desire for alcohol or drugs or sex or whatever, but they may have no control over that desire and, indeed, they may

14. It has been defended in Tenenbaum, *Appearance of the Good* and Oderberg, *The Metaphysics of Good and Evil*.

15. Cited by Pinsent in "Aquinas," 191.

16. Anscombe, *Intention*, 26–27. Anscombe might have to make some allowance for the skits of *Monty Python*, which include the thoroughly absurd.

even hate their desire or need for a substance. Such cases may be interpreted as involuntary and not free. The horror of addiction is, in part, that it can be like a form of slavery; the addict is someone trapped in a vicious cycle—and, of course, it can create a horror for the family and co-workers of the addict who is not acting on the basis of real goods.[17]

This guise of the good thesis challenges a popular view that evil is more interesting and powerful than that which is good. When we consider a stereotypical catalog of evil persons in history (Hitler, Stalin, Mao, Pol Pot, Charles Manson) or in fiction (Darth Vader, Voldemort, Sauron, the Joker, Dracula), don't we fear them because of their great, evil power? Perhaps this is so, but, consider just one case: didn't Hitler present himself as a great savior who would right the wrongs of Germany's defeat in the Great War, that he would exterminate those who threatened the great good of Arian blood purity? Of course, most of the modern world knows how such "goods" are not authentic goods, but would he have achieved power without convincing his followers that they were achieving a good worth killing (and even dying) for?

I commend to you a guise of the good thesis, while acknowledging that evil is real and that, while evildoing involves the damaging of something good, evil can take the form of very real, malignant, life-destroying hatred. Persons have killed others in cold blood, relishing the destruction of innocent children and the sustained torture of persons of different races, tribes, genders, religions, and nation-states. Now, it may be (indeed, I suspect it is true) that the evil-doers might tell themselves that their actions are permissible for some hideous, twisted reason (e.g., they

17. Maybe an addict can be seen as seeking the relief from the pain of withdrawal, which can be understood as a kind of good, albeit very temporary and unhealthy.

are exacting revenge for past harms or, more radically, they have embraced a nihilism according to which their victims are worthless and expendable), but that does not make them any less evil.

ORIGINAL SIN AND FREE WILL

Before moving on to the topic of redemption and justification, let us reflect on the Christian view of evil in light of the theology of original sin and free will.

Historically, Christian philosophers and theologians have taken different views of original sin.

Augustine championed a literal reading of the Edenic narrative in Genesis according to which we were created in paradise, the Garden of Eden. The original sin of Adam and Eve places a curse or punishment not only upon them but also upon us, their descendants, who are considered to be in some sense present "in" our primal ancestors. Thus, the entire human race faces the consequences of the disobedience in Eden. For Augustine, original sin meant that (a) all humans are held accountable for the primal sin and are justly punished for it, and (b) our natures have been corrupted such that we cannot resist sin's gravitational pull. Claim (a) is in some tension with later biblical passages (e.g., "The one who sins is the one who will die"; Ezekiel 18:20) and our moral intuition that it would be wrong to blame an innocent child for the sin of a parent, let alone a distant ancestor. Then again, it seems that there is an inevitable way in which biological beings such as ourselves will naturally impact our descendants. While this does not mean that our descendants would inherit guilt, it would mean that they inherit some liabilities; "original sin" refers to the origin of sin, it does not *ipso facto* refer to the perpetuation of guilt. We can make sense of ancestral wrongdoing as infecting the moral standing of descendants. If my ancestors were slave-owners and I benefited greatly from the institution of slavery, it seems that I owe some restitution to those descendants of the slaves my family claimed to own. (I put this in terms of a claim, because the injustice of enslavement means that the "owners" did not truly own other people; instead, "masters" were unjustly exploiting people who, by nature, are free and should thus have their freedom respected legally, politically, and religiously.) As I write this chapter, we in the United States are having a major national conversation about white privilege. An Augustinian would be theologically very much at home with this debate. Augustine would contend that while current, privileged white persons are not themselves guilty for past wrongs, they nonetheless inherit the benefits of past wrongs and thus they inherit the duty to redress and rectify the effects of past injustice.

There is another Christian tradition about original sin that would share the idea that we can inherit unjust benefits, but does not envisage the original sin as an expulsion from paradise. St. Irenaeus of Lyon proposes that God created human beings as immature, childish creatures who were almost inevitably going to do wrong. Rather than creation being a story of a fall from perfection, the creation of humans is more of an evolution in which we go from selfish, immature creatures to mature, ideally unselfish creatures who are, over time, morally and spiritually transformed into living in harmony with God.[18]

Whether Christians follow Augustine or Irenaeus or another model of original sin, they must hold that we

18. The greatest representative of this approach to evil is John Hick in *Evil and the God of Love*. For a helpful guide to other views of original sin, see Stump and Meister, eds., *Original Sin and the Fall: Five Views*.

have one of the conditions that make us responsible for our lives: *free will*. The freedom we have is not absolute or unrestricted; obviously, each of us is born into various constrained circumstances. What is perhaps most obvious is that being human itself has restraints and confining conditions. We are not free to fly (unaided) or to live very long without oxygen. Moreover, the exercise of freedom requires imagination: for you to freely do X, you have to be able to imagine not doing X.

Why would a Christian think we possess a free will? I suggest that our conviction that we have freedom is based on our common sense and on everyday experiences of ourselves as agents. Exercising our power to choose might sometimes feel like a passive event (for example, you look at a restaurant menu and it simply occurs to you that you want scallops), but when we act deliberately in the presence of alternatives, I believe that this is typically borne out in experience of our exercising power when there is more than one possible future.[19] The case for believing we possess free will was vexing in the context of a deterministic, scientific worldview, but today's physics, specifically quantum mechanics, now recognizes some indeterminacy in the natural world. Of course, just because there is indeterminacy (that is, not every event that occurs happens necessarily given the laws of nature and antecedent conditions) does not mean that persons have free will, but recognizing indeterminacy removes one obstacle to trusting our own experience.

For the record, the view I am commending here is called *incompatibilism*, the thesis that freely chosen acts cannot be *completely determined* by either nature or nurture, though they may be *influenced* by both. The view that free will and determinism are compatible is called—no

19. See Taliaferro and Meister, *Contemporary Philosophical Theology*, chapter 7.

surprises here—*compatibilism*. Some prominent Christian theologians, such as Jonathan Edwards, have embraced compatibilism, and some Christians, such as Martin Luther, have even denied that we have the radical power of free will. I am advocating for an alternative path to both Edwards and Luther.

One reason to affirm an incompatibilist view of free will is that it more easily allows persons to claim moral responsibility for their actions and characters; we were not predetermined to be the sorts of persons we are. Among contemporary philosophers, Alvin Plantinga is the most well-known for embracing the view that God has given us free will and, in so doing, God cannot determine our actions. When God creates a creature that is truly free to do either good or evil, God cannot fix things so that the creature only does what is good:

> A world containing creatures who are significantly free (and freely perform more good than evil actions) is more valuable, all else being equal, than a world containing no free creatures at all. Now God can create free creatures, but He can't *cause* or *determine* them to do only what is right. For if He does so, then they aren't significantly free after all; they do not do what is right *freely*. To create creatures capable of *moral good*, therefore, He must create creatures capable of moral evil; and He can't give these creatures the freedom to perform evil and at the same time prevent them from doing so. As it turned out, sadly enough, some of the free creatures God created went wrong in the exercise of their freedom; this is the source of moral evil. The fact that free creatures sometimes go wrong, however, counts neither against God's omnipotence nor against His goodness; for He could have

forestalled the occurrence of moral evil only by removing the possibility of moral good.[20]

We will see in future chapters the importance of freedom from the standpoint of a Christian guide to evil.

QUESTIONS FOR DISCUSSION

1. If we believe that nature is good, what are we to make of death and suffering? It seems that death and decay are natural. Christians have held different views. There are some biblical and deuterocanonical texts that suggest that God did not create death, nor does God desire the death of creatures. Consider the Book of Wisdom 1:12–14:

   Do not bring on your own death by sinful actions. God did not invent death, and when living creatures die, it gives him no pleasure. He created everything so that it might continue to exist, and everything he created is wholesome and good. There is no deadly poison in them. No, death does not rule this world.

   The subject of life after life is taken up at the end of chapter 2. Consider your own view on the nature of death—when, if ever, might death be good or natural?

20. Plantinga, *The Nature of Necessity*, 166–67. Christian philosophers have differed on whether they believe future free actions can be foreknown by God or any mind, no matter how great, on the grounds that prior to a creature making a free choice there is no fact of the matter about what the free agent will do. This viewpoint is sometimes linked to what is called *presentism* (only the present is real, though there are truths about the past) and *open theism*, the idea that, even for God, the future is open (not pre-determined). See Rice, *The Future of Open Theism*.

2. Are there beings whose very nature is evil? What about some parasites that seem to destroy their hosts? (For a slightly amusing treatment of whether there might be cases in the natural world of sexual cannibalism, see David Oderberg's *The Metaphysics of Good and Evil*, chapter 4.)

3. Some people try to justify God's allowing of evils in creation by arguing that, despite appearances, in the end such evils contribute to the larger good of the whole cosmos. But if that is so does it not make those evils into goods, thereby not so much *explaining* the evils as *explaining them away*?

2

THE DIFFERENCE BETWEEN JUSTIFICATION AND REDEMPTION

PROVISIONAL DISTINCTIONS

MOST OF US RECOGNIZE that evil comes in different orders of magnitude. While in chapter 4 we will consider a Christian teaching that one should not do evil to fight or prevent evil, many of us think that it is permissible to do some wrongs to prevent greater ones. To take a textbook example: Imagine it is the Second World War and you are in German-occupied Europe, sheltering Jews in your home to prevent them from being taken to an extermination camp. The Gestapo knocks on your door and you are asked: "Tell me the full truth. Are you sheltering Jews in your home?" Most of us would think it permissible for you not to tell the truth. There are some ways to propose that deception, in this case, would not count as lying,[1] but for the present let us claim that not answering truthfully would be a lie and, as such, it would be wrong. But if any wrongdoing could be justified then surely this is a convincing case. If you agree, let us consider the rescuing of vulnerable, innocent persons as a *justificatory good*. Justificatory goods make a wrongdoing justified.[2] (And just to head off a potential confusion: when I speak of "justification" in this book I am *not* speaking of the doctrine of "justification by faith." Rather, I am referring to reasons that make a moral choice "justified" in the circumstances.)

Consider a different type of good, I will refer to as a *redemptive good*. Imagine a loving couple, Chris and Pat. All is well until one day Pat betrays their relationship by having an affair. Imagine Pat comes to realize the wrongness of the betrayal and seeks to be reconciled with Chris through a remorseful confession, a renouncing of his past act. (Pat sincerely and sorrowfully adjures any real or perceived good in the infidelity.) Pat gives evidence of repentance and begs for forgiveness and reconciliation. Imagine Chris has met another person and might find healing and a cherished intimacy in a new relationship. But instead of pursuing this other, promising relationship, imagine Chris forgives Pat and seeks reconciliation. OK, I admit this is not a terribly good short story, but I ask you to imagine that after their reconciliation Chris and Pat have a great good, which we might call *reconciliatory love*. I suggest that this might indeed be a great, even profound good, as it would

1. One famous option is to define a lie as deceiving someone who deserves the truth. Arguably, those seeking to hunt down people as part of a genocidal campaign do not deserve to be helped, let alone be aided by them being given accurate information.

2. For a stringent case against lying even to save thousands of innocent persons, see Griffith, *Lying*. For an excellent, more nuanced approach see Carson, *Lying*.

involve displaying love when the couple is at their worst. To be loved when you have done something embarrassing is good, but to be loved when you have done something horrific is an awesome act of love. To deeply reflect on this scenario, all sorts of things would need to be clarified about the nature of forgiveness (What is it? Is it always good?), but I think most readers will resonate with the idea that a profound experience of reconciliatory love can deepen one's own character and intimate relationships. In such a case, I propose that what we would have is a redemptive good, but not a justificatory good. That is, the good of reconciliatory love does not in any way overshadow or justify the betrayal. The betrayal remains bad, even evil. A reconciliatory good is in some respects more than a salvage operation. You might salvage good, working parts from your car after an accident. In the Chris and Pat saga, a relationship has been saved or salvaged, but it has also been transformed by Pat's moral or spiritual re-birth or renewal in turning away from wrong action and desire, and by Chris's gift of accepting Pat back into an intimate, loving relationship.[3]

JUSTIFICATORY GOODS AND REDEMPTIVE GOODS

The difference between justificatory and redemptive goods may be found throughout the Bible and the history of Christianity. It is a vital component of an early, classic biblical narrative: Noah and the flood. In Genesis 6–8 humankind is judged to be thoroughly wicked. God sets

3. As a personal note, referring back to my autobiographical paragraph in the introduction, I think my life as an adult person of faith was deepened (and thus my life redeemed) by my return to faith after spending some of my youth in philosophical and material destitution.

out to destroy the wicked with a mighty flood while saving Noah, his family, and animals in an Ark. The story has many layers and a long history: for example, later Christian commentators have interpreted the Ark as a foreshadowing of the church (which is why some churches have been shaped like a ship; when parishioners look up at exposed wooden beams, it is as though one is looking at the bottom of a ship, the keel). If you judge the part about God destroying the earth (including those animals not rescued on the Ark) as unworthy of an unsurpassable good God, then on Augustinian grounds you may treat the story as a kind of parable or lesson. One lesson, appropriate in a theology of creation, is that human wickedness can impair the planet, including nonhuman animal and plant life. The lesson that is relevant in this chapter is the theological tenet that if God were to exact punishment for the wickedness in this world and in this life, none of us would live. God instead establishes a covenant with Noah—this is sometimes referred to as the Noahic covenant. In this covenant, God sets aside an exacting, retributive punishment of persons in this life. Punishment and reward are not utterly forsworn but are seen in terms of *aspiration* and *eschatology*. Both concepts enter into interpreting biblical proverbs about the fate of the wicked and the righteous: "Be sure of this: the wicked will not go unpunished, but those who are righteous will go free" (Proverbs 11:21). Seen from the standpoint of the Noahic covenant, such proverbs are interpreted as advancing two teachings. First, we should aspire to see the wicked punished in this life and the righteous rewarded, yet this is not something that God will bring about through dramatic events in human history. Second, the wicked will be punished, as they should be, but perhaps not in this life but in life after this life. Teachings about life after life are part of eschatology (from the Greek *eschatos*, meaning "end," and *logos*, which can mean "logic" or "word"), which takes into account the so-called Last Things, which includes New Testament prophecy about *the end of the age and the dawning of the new age.*

It is the Noahic covenant that theologically grounds the idea that in this life, not all suffering is punishment. It is the Noahic covenant that makes the biblical book of Job possible. In that book, Job is an innocent person who undergoes great suffering. His innocence is part of the reason why some Christians have seen Job as a type or foreshadowing of Jesus Christ.

The Noahic covenant compels one to consider the relationship between justice and mercy. According to one historically important line of thought, mercy and justice are in conflict. Justice requires that persons get what they deserve, whether this be in terms of reward or punishment, while mercy is often interpreted as undeserved favor. A this-world case would be one in which a magistrate is bound by justice to inflict some heavy penalty (maybe even the death penalty) on a criminal, but for the sake of some good does not do so. Perhaps the magistrate has mercy because the criminal has repented and can be an agent for public service, even persuading other wrongdoers to repent. From a Christian point of view, what is the good that might come through God's mercy and God's postponement or superseding of justice in this life? For Christians, this is the hope of redemption: the restoring and reconciling of evildoers who turn from evil toward the good.

THE REDEMPTION OF THE WORLD

Let's step back and connect the concept of redemption with what we explored in chapter 1 about human nature. According to many, perhaps most Christian philosophers,

the goal or purpose of human nature is happiness or fulfill-
ment. I will cite just two preeminent Christian thinkers on
this, beginning with Boethius:

> The whole concern of men, which the effort of a
> multitude of pursuits keeps busy, moves by dif-
> ferent roads, yet strives to arrive at one and the
> same end, that of happiness. . . . In all of these
> things it is obviously happiness alone that is de-
> sired; for whatever a man seeks above all else,
> that he reckons the highest good. But we have
> defined the highest good as happiness; where-
> fore each man judges that state to be happy
> which he desires above all others. . . . And you
> also, earthly creatures that you are, have some
> image, though hazy, in your dreams of your be-
> ginning; you see, though with a far from clear
> imagination yet with some idea, that true end of
> your happiness. Your natural inclinations draw
> you towards that end, to the true good.[4]

Anselm of Canterbury (1038–1109) offers a similar outlook:

> It ought not to be doubted that the nature of
> rational beings [was] created by God . . . in
> order that, through rejoicing in him, it might
> be blessedly happy. . . . Man, being rational by
> nature, was created . . . to the end that, through
> rejoicing in God, he might be blessedly happy.
> . . . God . . . [made us] for the purpose of eternal
> happiness.[5]

So, Boethius and Anselm underscore happiness as the
end of all, and Christian thinkers and artists have developed stunning portraits of a good, reconciling end.

---

4. Boethius, *The Consolation of Philosophy* (trans. D. R. Taylor),
233, 235, 241.

5. Anselm, *Anselm of Canterbury*, 315–16.

Consider this passage from William Langland's *Piers the Ploughman* on the reconciliation of mercy and truth:

> I drew back in the darkness and went to the depths of the earth. And there, in accordance with Scripture [Psalm 85:10], I dreamt that I saw a maiden come walking from the West, and looking towards hell. Mercy was her name, and she seemed a very gentle lady, courteous and kind in all she said. And then I saw her sister come walking quietly out of the East, and gazing intently westwards. She was very fair, and her name was Truth, for she possessed a heavenly power that made her fearless. . . . "I give way," said Truth, "You are in the right, Mercy. Let us make our peace together, and seal it with a kiss."[6]

So, how do we get from evildoing to this great end, the end of repentance and reconciliation? From a Christian point of view, this involves our being responsive to the reality of the living God in space and time as revealed by prophets, sacred events, and texts, but ultimately atonement with God happens through the incarnate life of Jesus of Nazareth.

A few words about the incarnation, and then back to the subject of redemption. How can God, the creator and sustainer of the cosmos, who is omnipresent, omnipotent, omniscient, necessarily existing, essentially good, timeless (or without temporal beginning or end), became incarnate as a contingent, finite, weak, often ignorant human being, who was born and died in a remote region of the Roman Empire? I suggest that it is appreciating the magnitude of divine attributes that enable us to form an idea of how an

6. William Langland, *Piers the Ploughman* (trans. J. F. Goodridge), 220–29.

incarnation might occur. Being a human being involves breathing, thinking, feeling, sensing, eating, drinking, acting, and so on, in and through our bodies; our liabilities to being hurt or satiated, being hungry or nourished all takes place in our embodiment. In traditional Christology (theology about Jesus Christ), the Second Person of the Trinity (God the Son) limits the divine consciousness, creating an embodiment such that the Second Person of the Trinity breathes, thinks, feels, senses, eats, drinks, and acts in the embodied Jesus of Nazareth who was born, lived, taught, healed, was arrested, tortured, crucified, and rose from the dead. Orthodox Christian tradition insisted on the reality of the incarnation: Jesus was *wholly human*. This was at odds with first-century Gnosticism and Docetism, which envisaged Jesus as not really human. The tradition also affirms that Jesus is *wholly God* (*totus Deus*) but not the whole of God (*totum Dei*). It is precisely because the triune God is omnipotent (all-powerful) that God in the Second Person can become limited and focused in an embodied life without the whole of God becoming limited.

The extraordinary, dramatic nature of the incarnation may be appreciated by comparing it to the way we ourselves can become intimately present to one another in sexual intimacy. Lest you think I am introducing some novel theological pornography, I note straightaway that Christians have long interpreted the erotic love poem in the Bible, the Song of Songs, as an allegory of the love between God and the soul. And important theologians such as Origin and St. Bernard of Clairvaux have interpreted the poem as showing us God's love for us in the incarnation. In the following passage from the book *Sexual Desire: A Philosophical Investigation*, Roger Scruton compares the Christian view of the incarnation with his account of how two persons become incarnate with and for each other in sexual interplay:

That, I believe, is the real mystery of incarnation. It is part of the genius of Christianity that it invites us to understand the relation between God and his creation in terms of a mystery that we have, so to speak, continually between our hands. The mystery that we confront in the sexual act, we can neither resolve nor abjure. No first-person perspective can bear the identity of a person, nor can it be united with the only thing—the body—in which individuality is revealed to us. And yet, so powerful is the paroxysm of desire that it seems to me as though the very transparency of your self is, for a moment, revealed on the surface of your body, in a mysterious union that can be touched but never comprehended. Those parts of the body which remain dark to me are dark only with the shadow cast by the flame of your self. This burning of the soul in the flesh—the *llama de amor viva* [living flame of love] of St John of the Cross—is the symbol of all mystic unions, and the true reason for the identity of imagery between the poetry of desire and the poetry of worship. The unity which I endeavour to elicit from you is one which I seek also to enact in myself. We are engaged in an impossible but necessary enterprise. We are attempting to unite our bodies with a non-existent "owner," who is unable to possess the individuality for which he craves, but who sustains the illusion of his own existence, as a reflection in the glass of another's eye. In this resides the true significance of the "involuntary" self-expressions which, I argued, form the initial focus of desire. The smile that draws me on is of flesh and blood. The desire to kiss it is the desire to plant my lips, not to a mouth, but to a smile: to a portion of the body into which I have summoned the other's perspective. A smile is indeed

41

the food of love, while a mouth can be the food of love only for someone whose rage has turned desire to appetite.[7]

As a side note, when Scruton wrote this passage he was not a Christian, but he came to Christian faith some years later.

I bring to your attention one other portrait of the incarnation in a romantic context. This one is a story of a king and a maiden, as told by Søren Kierkegaard:

Suppose there was a king who loved a humble maiden. The king was like no other king. Every statesman trembled before his power. No one dared breathe a word against him, for he had the strength to crush all opponents.

And yet this mighty king was melted by love for a humble maiden who lived in a poor village in his kingdom. How could he declare his love for her? In an odd sort of way, his kingliness tied his hands. If he brought her to the palace and crowned her head with jewels and clothed her body in royal robes, she would surely not resist—no one dared resist him. But would she love him?

She would say she loved him, of course, but would she truly? Or would she live with him in fear, nursing a private grief for the life she had left behind? Would she be happy at his side? How could he know for sure? If he rode to her forest cottage in his royal carriage, with an armed escort waving bright banners, that too would overwhelm her. He did not want a cringing subject. He wanted a lover, an equal. He wanted her to forget that he was a king and she a humble maiden and to let shared love cross the

7. Scruton, *Sexual Desire*, 128.

gulf between them. For it is only in love that the unequal can be made equal.

The king, convinced he could not elevate the maiden without crushing her freedom, resolved to descend to her. Clothed as a beggar, he approached her cottage with a worn cloak fluttering loose about him. This was not just a disguise—the king took on a totally new identity—He had renounced his throne to declare his love and to win hers.[8]

I recommend some recent, promising work on the philosophy of the incarnation.[9]

So, how might the incarnation be an instrument of atonement and redemption? What is the main element missing in the short tale of Chris and Pat? In virtually all wrongdoings, restitution can only be partial. If I have betrayed in our relationship, we might settle on an amount of money that would appease your anger, but I cannot give you back the time you wasted in our relationship. Over the years I have studied major cases of apologies. Among the more remarkable are cases in which the wrongdoer is led to say, "If I could turn back time, I would not have done what I did." Some wrongdoers have said, "If I could change history, I would." Consider two examples. When South African President F. W. de Klerk expressed regret about apartheid he announced: "Deep regret goes much further than saying you are sorry. Deep regret says that if I could turn the clock back, and if I could do anything about it, I would like to have avoided it."[10] When Kevin Gover, assistant secretary

8. Kierkegaard, *Provocations*, 93–95.

9. See Swinburne, *The Christian God*; Morris, *The Logic of God Incarnate*; Cross, *The Metaphysics of the Incarnation*; Adams, *Christ and Horrors*.

10. Cited by Lazare, *On Apology*, 109.

of the Bureau of Indian Affairs for the U.S. Department of Interior apologized on behalf of his agency on their abuse of Native Americans, saying: "Let us begin by expressing our profound sorrow for what this agency has done in the past. Just like you, when we think of these misdeeds and their tragic consequences, our hearts break and our grief is as pure and complete as yours. We desperately wish we could change history, but of course we cannot."[11] Frankly, I find these expressions illuminating as they speak to the depth of the apology, the renunciation of the past, and a deep yearning for the impossible: to erase the past or to fully make up for the past. Consider the reverse: someone is so unrepentant that they charge that if time were reversed, they would do exactly the same thing. The later would solidify the past, whereas a repentant soul is seeking to undo the harm they made.

All this relates to the incarnation, for Christians believe that Christ took on the suffering of the world. In response to his proclamation of the kingdom of God with healing miracles, he was met with scorn and, ultimately, his message rejected, he was tortured, crucified, died, buried, and then rose again from the dead. Some contemporary Christians may be embarrassed about belief in miracles and perhaps prefer a more "metaphorical" interpretation of events; for example, believing Christ rose from the dead meant that the followers of Christ felt that he lives on in their faith. I suggest that, whatever we want to believe now, it is virtually impossible to deny that there is very early historical testimony that Christ rose from the dead in a bodily resurrection and appeared to many.[12] They may have

11. Cited by Lazare, *On Apology*, 109–10.

12. See N. T. Wright, *The Resurrection of the Son of God*; Swinburne's *The Resurrection of the Son of God*; and Davis, "The Gospels Are Reliable as Historically Factual Accounts."

been mistaken, but the fact of the early Christian claims to be eye-witnesses of the resurrected Christ is hard to deny. Positing only a metaphorical "resurrection" does not do justice to the profound growth of the church and the many Christians who were prepared to die for their belief in the resurrected Lord. In my view, skepticism about the historical reliability of the New Testament is often fueled by presupposing some form of naturalism (there is no God, but only nature, unbroken natural laws). Once one approaches the New Testament with an open mind about theism and divine revelation, historical evidence of the fact of the resurrection becomes persuasive.[13] I do not claim the evidence is compelling insofar as I am not asserting that all impartial scholars who are open, in principle, to theistic explanations will reach the same conclusion about the New Testament's reliability; and yet I do suggest the evidence makes such a conclusion reasonable.

The resurrection of Jesus Christ is taken by many Christian philosophers and theologians as God's promise of resurrection or life with God beyond death. Many texts in the New Testament urge us to become united with Christ spiritually as this leads us to greater life here and now as well as an ultimate life eschatologically (John 11:25–26; Romans 6:5; 1 Corinthians 6:14). Especially in the Gospel of John, the relationship with Christ is described in terms of irrepressible, unconquerable, abundant life. The Greek terms for life (*zoe, psyche,* and *bios*) are used forty-seven times in that gospel. One way in which the incarnation is believed to lead to redemption is by providing a means by which the ravages of sin may be overcome through

13. See Earman, *Hume's Abject Failure*; Keener, *The Credibility of the New Testament*; and Twelftree, ed., *The Cambridge Companion to Miracles*. One of the most thorough defenses of the credibility of miracles is a two-volume work, *Miracles,* by Craig Keener.

reconciliation with others and with God in a transcendent life. This understanding of redemption is referred to as the *Christus Victor* account.[14] On this account, the life and work of Christ provide the means by which we can come to the happiness described by Boethius and Aquinas.

There are other models of redemption in a Christian tradition that are historically important, and more than one model may be adopted; they are not incompatible. A very popular model, developed by Anselm, is that Christ bears the penalty or cost of our sins on our behalf. Christ's suffering and death can constitute a vicarious offering for us, offering to God a gift of infinite love. (This model has troubled some as it involves an innocent person [Jesus] bearing an undeserved penalty [we deserve death, not Jesus], but I believe it has some merit. You might wrongly injure someone who would have died but for a good Samaritan who intervenes, giving her life to save the person you harmed [imagine the Samaritan gives a blood transfusion that leads to her death]. In a sense, you might have deserved the death penalty for murder except for the Samaritan's giving her life to rescue the one injured.) There is a subjective model of atonement, associated with the philosopher Abelard, according to which the incarnation, life, and resurrection of Christ constitute an overwhelming display of divine love that moves people to repentance and to seek reconciliation with God.[15] Yet another model, advanced by Richard Swinburne, is that Jesus Christ's life constitutes a perfect offering or oblation to God and that we are saved by joining in this offering.[16] Eleonore Stump has defended an account of redemption that involves our linking ourselves with the love of God revealed in the life (and continued presence)

14. This is well articulated by Gustaf Aulén in *Christus Victor*.

15. Abelard, "Exposition of the Epistle to the Romans."

16. Swinburne, *Responsibility and Atonement*.

of Jesus, delivering us from our self-centered guilt and shame.[17] There are still other models of redemption.[18]

Hell and Heaven

What is the modern theological thought on hell? There are abundant alternatives. One might think of hell and heaven as mythological, yet important symbols of evil and goodness. In the next chapter, I will suggest that addressing the problem of evil from a Christian point of view requires that there is more than this life in which redemption takes place. Today and throughout human history, too many lives are cut short or lived out with enormous suffering and disability such that a loving, super-abundant good God would not let death have the last say. More on this soon. The other options: there are current defenses of the view that eternal separation from God may be one of the outcomes of God truly giving and respecting the freedom of creatures.[19] If you wish to forever refuse a relationship with God, that may be up to you. Traditionally this eternal separation was a condition of everlasting torment. However, hell, conceived of as a place of unending suffering, does not seem in keeping with the task of the redemption of the wicked by God. Another view is *universalism*, the view that all persons will ultimately come to be in relation with God.[20] A middle position would be a kind of contingent universalism: all will have the opportunity to be in harmony with God, and this might well

---

17. Stump, *Atonement*. See also Stump, *Wandering in Darkness*.

18. See Sykes, ed., *Sacrifice and Redemption*.

19. See Walls, *Hell: The Logic of Damnation*.

20. See Hick, *Evil and the God of Love*; Talbott, *The Inescapable Love of God*; MacDonald, *The Evangelical Universalist*; Reitan and Kronen, *God's Final Victory*; Hart, *That All Shall Be Saved*.

involve all persons (but this is not necessitated).[21] Another view that some adopt is *annihilationism*: if a person steadfastly refuses to be in harmony with God, God will allow them to cease to be.[22] Annihilationism and contingent universalism both give a high place to the importance of freedom. This is in accord with the idea that hell is self-created, as opposed to a domain like a prison that God created to place the damned. These alternatives—eternal torment, annihilation, and universalism—can each be found in the first three centuries of Christian tradition.

How should we handle traditional notions of hell and heaven? I suggest that hell and heaven might be thought of the way the Gospel of John treats life: one may be in hell or heaven now in this life as well as in life beyond this life.[23] Hell is traditionally thought of as life that is separated from God; this is somewhat problematic as, according to Christianity, there can be no place where God is not present. Still, one may be in a state where God is present while one outright rejects any harmony with God. Those theologians who adopt this view of hell describe the suffering of hell as the rejecting of divine love. The seventh-century theologian Isaac of Nineveh writes:

> As for me, I say that those who are tormented
> in hell are tormented by the invasion of love.
> What is there more bitter and more violent that
> than the pains of love? Those who feel that they
> have sinned against love bear in themselves a

21. See Walls, ed., *The Oxford Handbook of Eschatology*, Part II, chapters 11–17.

22. For a through treatment of annihilationism, see Griffith, *Decreation*.

23. This realized eschatology is evident in the fourth Gospel in verses like John 3:18 and 5:28–29 when the same Greek term *krinō* (judged/condemned) is used to refer to our present condition as well as to the eschatological climax of that condition.

damnation much heavier than the most dreaded punishments. The suffering with which sinning against love afflicts the heart is more keenly felt than any other torment. It is absurd to suppose that sinners in hell are deprived of God's love. Love . . . is offered impartially. But by its very power it acts in two ways. It torments sinners, as happens here on earth when we are tormented in the presence of a friend to whom we have been unfaithful. And it gives joy to those who have been faithful.[24]

Isaac of Nineveh held that God's compassion for those who are wicked would be stronger than any wickedness of creatures, suggesting that (eventually) God's compassion would win over all:

As is a grain of sand weighed against a large amount of gold, so, in God, is the demand for equitable judgment weighed against his compassion. As a handful of sand in the boundless ocean, so art the sins of the flesh in comparison with God's providence and mercy. As a copious spring could not be stopped up with a handful of dust, so the Creator's compassion cannot be conquered by the wickedness of creatures.[25]

Rather than think of hell as a prison (in which the wicked are relegated to a site cut off from the redeemed) or a guillotine (in which the wicked are annihilated), Isaac of Nineveh, Gregory Nyssen, and others imagine hell as a kind of hospital in which the dysfunction and impaired creatures are purged in light of a final redemption and reconciliation with the God of love.[26]

24. Cited in Clement, *The Roots of Christian Mysticism*, 303.

25. Clement, *The Roots of Christian Mysticism*, 306.

26. The three images here come from a lecture by Robin Parry.

Purgatory

Back to redemption, Christians have long held that God's love for us is not isolated to this life and that God "desires the salvation of all people" (1 Timothy 2:4). This has motivated Christians to at least long for all persons to come in harmony with God (or, in traditional language, for all to reach heaven), though it is pretty obvious that at the time of death, very few humans are perfect or anything like saints. It is perhaps for this reason that the belief in purgatory has been making a comeback theologically.[27] In this new look at purgatory, it is speculated that after death some purgation or cleansing would be fitting. Most Christians believe that there is an order of love (*Ordo Amoris*): we ought to love persons and things and some things more than others. We should not love wealth and prestige more than we love persons, for example. Punishment, which usually involves some suffering or privation, might be one means whereby we come to observe the horrors of what we have done and we become (perhaps by God's love, as seen by Isaac of Nineveh) transformed into union with God and creation.

As we come to the next chapter, we will consider whether an all-good God would create and sustain our cosmos, with all its evil. Before doing so, let us briefly look at the prospect of judging worlds.

BEST POSSIBLE WORLDS

Some philosophers have held that if there is a God of unsurpassable goodness and perfect power, God would create the best possible world. Anything less would be unjustifiable. This has led to two different conclusions: (a) despite appearances to the contrary, this cosmos *is* the best possible

27. See Walls, *Purgatory: The Logic of Total Transformation*.

cosmos, juxtaposed with (b) the denial that this is the best possible world and thus the denial that God exists.

Two responses are worth considering to these stark alternatives. First, given that it is good for there to be creatures with free will and the covenant with Noah, whether ours is the best possible world *may not be up to God.* When I am less than the best possible professor (or writer!), the world is a little worse, but I suspect the fault lies with me. There is another matter to consider: does the concept of the best possible world even make sense? Some have argued plausibly that the idea of there being a best possible world is like the idea that there can be a greatest possible number: there cannot be one. Imagine a very simple theory of values: there being happy people is good. How might we imagine a greatest possible world of happy people? It would seem that however many happy people God creates, God could always create one more happy person. Moreover, what about the concept of any one person being maximally happy? Perhaps there is an upper limit to happiness given our biology—maybe there is a limit beyond which if we were any happier we would lose consciousness. Perhaps, but then couldn't an omnipotent being make creatures with different bodies (and different laws of nature) who had much greater happiness than we can sustain?

I suggest that a Christian view of good and evil not be framed in terms of a single scale. Arguably, creation consists of a plentitude of different types of goods, the flourishing of plants and animals amount to diverse forms of life that have incomparable values (the flight of a bird, the speed of a lion, the mating of sealions). There is no single scale of goods.

Before moving on, let us pause to consider whether judging the concept of "a best possible world" to be like "a greatest number" (i.e., an absurdity), we should worry about thinking of God as the greatest possible being. If the former idea is incoherent, is the latter idea? I suggest these are different, considering some of the divine attributes. Divine omnipotence is not best thought of as the power to actualize infinitely many states of affairs— because there cannot be a greatest possible number, God (logically) cannot bring about the greatest possible number of states of affairs. Rather, omnipotence is better thought of as the power to bring about any possible state of affairs (compatible with God's goodness). Similarly, divine omniscience is not best thought of as God being able to know the greatest possible number of things because there cannot be a greatest possible number of things. God's maximal goodness can instead be conceived of as including God truly loving and caring for the creation. Love and care can come in degrees, but I suggest we naturally think of loving care as having a fitting, natural magnitude. For example, I believe I have loving care for my wife, Jil. Is it conceivable that I could or should have even more loving care than I do now (that I take double the delight I do in her paintings)? Possibly, but this would be odd. We might well locate a maximum in human love; the highest level is that we are willing to live for and with someone or, perhaps more radically, we are prepared to die for them. Back to God and maximal goodness: the Christian concept of God's goodness does include believing that God—in the incarnation—did live, die, and rise from the dead for us.

QUESTIONS FOR DISCUSSION

1. Think of some examples of goods that are justificatory or redemptive.

2. My preferred definition of forgiveness is that it involves the cessation of blame. If I keep blaming you for the injury, you may well conclude I have not (yet)

forgiven you. What do you think? Do you believe that a person needs to repent and ask for forgiveness prior to there being forgiveness? Can forgiveness sometimes be a duty?

3. Some object to the penal substitution model of redemption as it involves an innocent person suffering in the place of another. We seem to allow for some penal substitutions (e.g., I pay for your parking ticket) but not others (e.g., if I am sentenced to life in prison for murder, it does not seem acceptable for another person to serve the sentence). But perhaps Jesus's life, death, and resurrection might still be a kind of substitution in which Jesus undergoes redemptive suffering for our sake. In ordinary circumstances, we recognize that some people can undergo hardships for the sake of others (soldiers, firefighters). Do you think this helps us to understand the death of Christ?

4. In what respects might one use a metaphor (or model) of redemption in which Jesus is understood as fighting a battle on our behalf or rescuing us from sin and death?

5. Even if there is no such thing as "the best possible world" might there still be worlds that an all-good God could not create and, if so, what kinds of worlds would these be and why could God not create them?

6. Do you think the idea of ongoing purification and moral transformation after death is helpful? Why or why not?

7. Which of the views of 'hell' discussed in this chapter do you find the most helpful and which the most objectionable? Why?

3

THE ETHICS OF CREATING A WORLD AND THE ETHICS IN A WORLD

PROVISIONAL DISTINCTIONS

IF A BYSTANDER WITNESSES an assault being committed against an innocent person and they do not try to rescue the person in distress, aren't they partly responsible for the harm done? Imagine the bystander is very powerful, knows how to disarm the assailant, and can rescue the victim with ease. Most of us would think that the bystander *ought* to intervene and would be culpable for not doing so. If that is so, what do we think about an omnipresent, omnipotent, omniscient agent in a world full of suffering? Is God a guilty bystander?

There are various responses to this problem of evil; some Christian philosophers, such as Brian Davies, deny that God is a moral agent. Davies claims that God is indeed all good, but God is not a personal agent like us. He claims that to be a personal agent you have to be subject to duties and obligations that involve higher, binding laws and such higher laws make no sense when it comes to God. (For nothing is higher than or prior to God.) God thus has no moral obligations to creation. Maybe so, but there appear to be abundant biblical passages describing God in terms of God's loving action (John 3:16, God is described as loving the world and giving God's Son) and it is hard to think of God creating, conserving, and redeeming without this involving personal agency. Others deny that God is omnipotent: there is a telling book with the title *Omnipotence, and Other Theological Mistakes* by Charles Hartshorne. Process theologians and Boston personalists speculate that God is very powerful, but not *all* powerful, not *omni*potent. And some deny or restrict divine omniscience. Those described as open theists have claimed that God cannot know the future free acts of creatures (because they are by definition non-determined and so not predictable on the basis of our knowledge of the present). Thus, God literally takes a *risk* when creating the world because he does not know what the precise consequences will be. These limits of divine power and knowledge might be thought to help explain the presence of evil in the world. But what if we retain traditional, Christian theism? That is, what if we wish to retain belief in divine omnipotence and omniscience?

One option is to distinguish between the ethics of God creating a world and the ethics within a world. In this chapter let us consider what seems to be good and evil in our world (or, to put things differently, in reality), ultimately leading to the question of whether our world is or is not the kind of world that would be created and sustained by the God of Christianity. When heading into taking a kind of inventory of the good and evil around us, it should be noted that the God of Christianity is not a bystander, as Alvin Plantinga puts forcefully:

> As the Christian sees things, God does not stand idly by, coolly observing the suffering of his creatures. He enters into and shares our suffering. He endures the anguish of seeing his Son, the second person of the Trinity, consigned to the bitter, cruel, and shameful death on the cross. Some theologians claim that God cannot suffer. I believe they are wrong. God's capacity for suffering, I believe, is proportional to his greatness; it exceeds our capacity for suffering in the same measure as his capacity for knowledge exceeds ours. Christ was prepared to endure the agonies of hell itself; and God, the Lord of the universe, was prepared to endure the suffering consequent upon his Son's humiliation and death. He was prepared to accept this suffering in order to overcome sin, and death, and the evils that afflict our world, and to confer on us a life more glorious than we can imagine.[1]

We also do well to remember a point made in the introduction. The predominant Christian view on evil is that it should not take place, as John Hick makes explicit:

> What does that ultimate purpose mean for Auschwitz and Belsen and the other camps in which, between 1942 and 1945, between four and six million Jewish men, women and children were deliberately and scientifically murdered? Was this in any sense willed by God?

---

1. Plantinga, "Self-Profile," 36. Plantinga's claim depends upon the idea that God is passible, which means that God can be affected by what happens in creation. Divine passibilism is controversial in theology. I have defended it in *Consciousness and the Mind of God*.

The answer is obviously no. These events were utterly evil, wicked, devilish and, so far as the human mind can reach, unforgivable: they are wrongs that can never be righted, horrors which will disfigure the universe to the end of time, and in relation to which no condemnation can be strong enough, no revulsion adequate. It would have been better—much much better—if they had never happened. Most certainly God did not want those who committed these fearful crimes against humanity to act as they did. His purpose for the world was retarded by them and power of evil within it increased.[2]

AN INVENTORY OF GOODS

In assessing the goods of our cosmos, we may begin with the bare fact that there is a cosmos at all. I suggest that there is nothing inevitable in the existence of a cosmos of stars, planets, and stable laws of nature that have enabled the emergence of life. If gravity had been absent or weaker, there is reason to believe that no stars, planets, or galaxies would have formed. There is an impressive argument that the cosmos had to be finely tuned (with just the right strength of nuclear forces, say) in order to be life-sustaining, as it is today.[3] The process of evolution seems to generate great goods, and perhaps this has inevitably involved much suffering and destruction, as Keith Ward notes.

> In some possible universes, including this one, it could well be that some suffering is inevitable. Modern science helps us to see this. If humans have evolved in our universe from a primeval big

2. Hick, *Evil and the God of Love*, 361.
3. See Collins, "The Fine Tuning of the Cosmos Is Convincing."

bang, then that process of evolution necessarily involves suffering and destruction. Stars had to explode to form the heavier elements of which life is composed. Millions of organisms had to die in order for human life to evolve on this planet. Even now, humans have to destroy plant or animal life in order to survive. The physical laws of this universe depend upon destruction, mutation, conflict, and, therefore, destruction and death, if intelligent persons are to evolve in it. If we understood the laws of nature fully, we would see that such destruction and the suffering conscious beings feel when involved in it are inevitable consequences of having a universe like this.[4]

While many Christians today believe that God used evolution as a means of creating diverse species, some Christians in the nineteenth century objected, not simply on a literal interpretation of the opening chapters of Genesis, but on moral grounds. They argued that God would have used special creation that did not involve the kind of suffering that Charles Darwin seemed to have uncovered.[5] Today, we see a more holistic ecology highlighting symbiosis and inter-dependency that has yielded a view of nature that is not quite as horrifying as it was to Darwin's Victorian contemporaries.[6]

We need not see the evolution of human beings as the goal of evolution (or God's creation); many Christians today affirm the good of the whole natural world, especially the biosphere. We human beings have not lived up to the name of our species (*homo sapiens* means the *wise species*,

4. Ward, *The Big Questions in Science and Religion*, 79.

5. Jil Evans and I explore such concerns in our co-edited book *Turning Images in Philosophy, Science, and Religion*.

6. See Rolston, *Genes, Genesis, and God*.

sapientiae being the Latin term for wisdom), but we have evolved to have the good powers outlined in chapter 1, including our powers to act freely, to exercise moral judgment, to have religious and aesthetic experiences (of beauty and ugliness), and to live interdependently whereby our welfare is contingent on each other. While in the next sections of this chapter we will consider whether such powers and interdependence are (all things considered) worth it, it seems that in a world of stable laws of nature, some injuries of each other would have to accompany the good of collective responsibility. John Hick speculates that a world free of the possibility of wrongful injury would border on the absurd:

> No one would ever injure anyone else; the murderer's knife would turn to paper or his bullets to thin air; the bank safe, robbed of a million dollars, would miraculously become filled with another million dollars; fraud, deceit, conspiracy, and treason would somehow always leave the fabric of society undamaged. . . . The reckless driver would never meet with disaster. There would be no need to work, since no harm could result from avoiding work; there would be no call to be concerned for others in time of need or danger, for in such a world there could be no real needs or dangers.[7]

Richard Swinburne makes a related point about the scope of human freedom:

> Without a significant amount of natural evil, we simply would not have the opportunity to show patience . . . on the heroic scale required for us to form heroically good characters. It is a great

7. Hick, *Philosophy of Religion*, 44–46.

good for us to be able, through free choice over time, to form such characters.[8]

Swinburne goes on about there being some reason why God would allow for considerable scope of freedom:

> The less [God] allows men to bring about large scale horrors, the less the freedom and respon- sibility he gives to them. What in effect the objection is asking is that a God should make a toy-world, a world where things matter, but not very much; where we can choose and our choices can make a small difference but the real choices remains God's. For he simply would not allow us the choice of doing real harm, or through our negligence, allow real harm to occur. He would be like an over-protective parent who will not let his child out of his sight for a moment.[9]

Wrapping up the great goods of our world we might include loving relations, family and friends, reproduction, work, play, making works of art, sexuality, exploration, dis- covery, education, farming, medicine, law-making. . . . To which may be added the myriad goods of non-human ani- mal life, plants, the profound beauty of the world on both the micro and macro scale.

Now, turning to the dark side . . . .

AN INVENTORY OF EVILS

Where to begin? The eleven million killed in the Holocaust (including six million Jews)? This has been an important, searing reference point for any reflection on God and evil. Why did not God intervene to save the people whose

8. Swinburne, *Providence and the Problem of Evil*, 169.

9. Swinburne, *The Existence of God*, 219.

covenant stretches back to Abraham? Why did not God prevent the 108 million total killed in the twentieth century from warfare? The very idea of making an inventory of evil in a short book is preposterous. It was daunting enough to have co-edited the six-volume *History of Evil* (referenced in the introduction). But to at least gesture of what an inventory would have to include: Estimates of those human beings killed by other human beings through our history have been put as high as one billion. Those dying of plague, drought, floods, tsunamis, earthquakes, and other natural disasters are astronomical. One drought in India in 1965 killed an estimated 1,500,000 people. Think, too, of the vast numbers of victims of rape, incest, enslavement, torture, all those who have suffocated from relentless oppression and exploitation. We humans have ravaged the natural world, making animals suffer in unspeakable torment and subject to mindless slaughter. There is also the torment that nonhuman animals inflict on each other. In addition, we might note the prevalence of disease and death afflicting both human and non-human life.

Recently, the Christian philosopher Marilyn Adams has focused on what she calls horrendous evils, evil that is so severe as to threaten the idea that there is any good to one's life at all:

> The rape of a woman and axing off her arms, psychophysical torture whose ultimate goal is the disintegration of personality, betrayal of one's deepest loyalties, cannibalizing one's own offspring, child abuse of the sort described by Ivan Karamazov, child pornography, parental incest, slow death by starvation, participation in the Nazi death camps, the explosion of nuclear bombs over populated areas, having to choose between which of one's children shall live and which be executed by terrorists, being the

accidental and/or unwitting agent of the disfig-
urement or death of those one loves best.[10]

One cannot help but be staggered by any or all such
cases. Consider the sheer magnitude of evident evil. Let us
grant that, for the sake of argument, some suffering and
injury are essential in a world in which there is moral de-
velopment. So, imagine John Hick is correct to question the
assumption that a world without suffering would be better
than our world:

> But such an assumption overlooks the fact that
> a world in which there can be no pain or suf-
> fering would also be one without moral choices
> and hence no possibility of moral growth and
> development. For in a situation in which no one
> can ever suffer injury or be liable to pain or suf-
> fering, no distinction would exist between right
> and wrong action. No action would be morally
> wrong, because no action could ever have harm-
> ful consequences; likewise, no action would be
> morally right in contrast to wrong. Whatever
> the values of such a world, its structure would
> not serve the purpose of allowing its inhabitants
> to develop from self-regarding animality to self-
> giving love.[11]

So *some* suffering is essential, but why such a *magnitude*
of evils, including acts of *horrific* evil? I suggest that con-
templating horrific evils can easily put one in two, conflict-
ing states of mind: one might either hope that the God of
Christianity exists or hope that this God does not exist.

One might hope the God of Christianity does not exist
because if God was real that would mean that while God

10. Adams, "Horrendous Evils and the Goodness of God,"
211–12.

11. Hick, *A John Hick Reader*, 98–99.

may not be the agent involved in directly bringing about horrific evils, God has created and is sustaining our world in which they take place. One may conclude that God is thereby unjust and may hope that there is not such an all-powerful, all-knowing, unjust deity. On the other hand, we might hope that the God of Christianity exists because only an omnipotent, loving God might possibly redeem persons (including some nonhuman animal persons, if there are any) from the awful wreckage of this world. This is why many theistic philosophers stress life after death as an alternative to naturalism (according to which there is no God, only nature). As Hick points out, "according to naturalism, the evil that has afflicted so much of human life is final and irrevocable as the victims have ceased to exist."[12] Rabbi and theologian Dan Cohn-Sherbok contends that Judaism offers an important alternative to naturalism:

> Yet without this belief [in an afterlife], it is simply impossible to make sense of the world as the creation of an all-good, all-powerful God. Without the eventual vindication of the righteous in Paradise, there is no way to sustain the belief in a providential God who watches over His chosen people. If death means extinction, there is no way to make sense of the claim that he loves and cherishes all those who died in the concentration camps—suffering and death would ultimately triumph over each of those who perished. But if there is eternal life in a World to Come, then there is hope that the righteous will share in a divine life. Moreover, the divine attribute of justice demands that the righteous of Israel who met their death as innocent victims of the Nazis will reap an everlasting reward. Here then is an answer to the religious perplexities of the

12. Hick, *The Fifth Dimension*, 23.

Holocaust. The promise of immortality offers a way of reconciling the belief in a loving and just God with the nightmare of the death camps. As we have seen, this hope sustained the Jewish people through centuries of suffering and martyrdom. Now that Jewry stands on the threshold of the twenty-first century, it must again serve as the fulcrum of religious beliefs.[13]

The Christian philosopher Keith Ward agrees:

Theism would be falsified if physical death was the end, for then there could be no justification for [or, rather, redemption of] the existence of this world. However, if one supposes that every sentient being has an endless existence, which offers the prospect of supreme happiness, it is surely true that the sorrows and troubles of this life will seem very small in comparison. Immortality, for animals as well as humans, is a necessary condition of any acceptable theodicy; that necessity, together with all the other arguments for God, is one of the main reasons for believing in immortality.[14]

So, I conclude this brief overview of the evils of our world with the suggestion that if *we had positive reasons for thinking that death is the absolute extinction of persons* and we had good reasons for doubting *the incarnation and redeeming power of Jesus Christ*, it would be hard to believe in the unsurpassable, powerful goodness of God. On the other hand, if (as I believe) we have some positive reasons to believe it is possible for there to be an all-loving God who redeems us through Christ in this life and life after this life, then matters change.

13. Cohn-Sherbok, "Jewish Faith and the Holocaust," 292–93.
14. Ward, *Rational Theology and the Creativity of God*, 201–2.

GOODS AND EVILS IN AND OF THE COSMOS

I offer the following very general portrait of the co-existence of the God of Christianity and the evils in the world:

> There is an omnipotent, omniscient, all-good
> God of perfect love who has created and sustains
> a cosmos of at least one hundred billion galaxies
> in which there are (perhaps uncountably) many
> planets, at least one of which sustains life (there
> may or not be others—perhaps many billions
> of others). All the elements of the cosmos, with
> their causal powers and liabilities, are dependent
> upon divine creation and conservation such that
> none of them would endure over time without
> God's causal powers. The cosmos appears to be
> marked by uniform, stable laws that we current-
> ly are discovering through physics, chemistry,
> and biology. The vastness and grandeur of this
> cosmos merits our awe and delight as something
> sublime and of extraordinary beauty. On earth,
> chemical bonding led to the emergence of life
> and through a long, complex evolutionary his-
> tory, there has emerged plant and animal life,
> the biota and abiota. Amid the multitude of
> nonhuman animal life, some developed and are
> developing powers of movement and sentience,
> and with some mammals including humans,
> there emerges persons (selves or subjects) who
> have powers of movement, a range of senses and
> feelings, memory, reason, the power to love or
> hate, fear and desire, and (eventually) powers
> to make moral judgments and to act in light of
> what seem to be right or wrong choices, in ac-
> cordance with virtues and vices. Some use these
> powers for the good and welfare of persons and
> other forms of life, which are beautiful ends, but
> some use their powers for profoundly ugly and

wrong ends. In this cosmos, there are good and beautiful friendships, families, adventures, creativity, and there are evil and ugly enemies, hateful rulers, and soul-destroying acts such as rape, torture, murder, enslavement. These evils are contrary to the will and nature of God, abhorrent to God's purpose in creation. The cosmos contains abundant goods, but also earthquakes, floods, droughts, diseases, wildfires, plagues. The damage caused is sometimes increased or decreased due to human factors, but sometime calamities occur unaffected by human action and inaction. God acts through prophets and other created agents to fight and prevent some evils, but not always. Thus, while God commands persons not to murder, and judges each murderer guilty of a heinous crime and sacrilege, God does not miraculously intervene to prevent every murder. God seeks to be revealed and in relationship with created persons through experiences and events, though prophets and sages. Ultimately, God enters the created order as Jesus Christ, fully human, fully God, who teaches about the goodness and love of God, justice and mercy, and heals many who suffer. Jesus Christ himself suffers and dies and is raised from the dead in order to bring about the redemption of all. God through Christ and in other persons and modes, may be experienced as the loving and good One who will sustain persons at death in order to offer an opportunity of redemption beyond this life.

I did not include nonhuman animals in the narrative so far as this needs some qualifications. Minimally the narrative should add that the world of nonhuman animals contains great goods, but also enormous suffering through disease and predation. What is obvious to me is that a great deal of animal suffering at the hands of humans is morally wrong and, I believe, contrary to the will and nature of God. I think that intensive, industrial farms are morally repugnant. But it is less clear to me whether it is wrong to raise some nonhuman animals humanely, allowing for free-ranging and so on, with a view to killing them for food and such like. It is also unclear to me whether natural predation is an evil. Partly because we lack precise knowledge of animal suffering.[15] There are some Christian philosophers, like Keith Ward and Chad Meister, who believe that some nonhuman animals are persons or person-like beings and that an all-good, loving God would provide life after death for them.

There are a host of different ways to respond to the Christian claim that the magnitude of evil in the cosmos is compatible with the goodness of God. One might claim to know it is false, because God and evil are straightforwardly incompatible, so the presence of *any amount* of evil is enough to demonstrate the non-existence of God. The claim to *know* that a given philosophy is false is rare these days, but it happens.[16] More modestly, one might either claim to *believe* it is false or *unreasonable*. On the other hand, one might claim to know the Christian view of evil is true or, again more modestly, believe it to be true or reasonable. The reasons for accepting a whole worldview are complex and often involve many strands. For example, there are extensive arguments for the truth of theism—the ontological, cosmological, teleological, moral arguments, an argument from the emergence of consciousness and from religious experience—and significant debate about whether evidence is actually needed in order to have a

15. See Murray, *Nature Red Tooth and Claw*.

16. Gary Gutting has a masterful book, *What Philosophy Can Do*, on this topic.

warranted worldview.[17] One should also note that there are positions in between affirming or denying Christian theism. Some philosophers have claimed that religious faith should be first and foremost thought of in terms of trust or hope in God, rather than belief; you may trust or hope that someone will rescue you (and you actually are rescued) even if (at the time) you do not actually believe the rescue will occur. There is also a view called *skeptical theism* that is worthy of attention. On this view, a theist may be skeptical about our chances of ever knowing *why* an all-good God might allow (or not quickly destroy) evil, but claim that this does not undermine her belief in God's goodness as it would be unreasonable for her (or, more generally, us) to expect to *know* what reason God might have for allowing or not destroying evil. There are still other positions, such as the theology of protest. In this view, one affirms (whether on the basis of faith or evidence) that the God of Christianity exists, but in the tradition of Jeremiah the prophet, one protests against God not acting justly. The theology of protest harkens back to the notion that the relationship with God for the Hebrew people was one of wrestling (the name "Israel" means "one who wrestles with God," Genesis 32:22–33) and not always abject submission. Indeed, the Old Testament or Hebrew Bible is a history of Israel's protest against God, not simply their worship of God.

We do well also to recall the personal nature of the Christian struggle with evil. Two of the greatest twentieth-century Christian writers published their personal anguish with loss: C. S. Lewis in *A Grief Observed* records his grief over the death of his wife, and Nicholas Wolterstorff in *Lament for a Son* mourns the death of his son at twenty-five years old. Most Christians believe that Jesus Christ himself

17. See the free online *Stanford Encyclopedia of Philosophy* entry "Philosophy of Religion" for an overview of such concerns.

experienced the agony of feeling abandoned by God. On the cross, he cries "My God. My God. Why have you forsaken me?" (Matthew 27:46; Mark 15:34). Even those very skeptical about the historical reliability of the New Testament have reason to believe in the accuracy of this event (often referred to as the cry of dereliction), for it shows Christ himself in a state of profound doubt and vulnerability. Followers of Jesus would probably prefer portraying their master as never being subject to doubt; the fact that this memory of Jesus's suffering of doubt was preserved rather than covered up is telling.

The Christian response to evil includes both theory and practice in confronting and overturning evil, the topic of the fourth chapter. But before turning in that direction, I offer some reflections on whether it is reasonable to hope or believe in life after this life. Given the importance of an afterlife for assessing the compatibility of the God of Christianity and evil, we should pause to consider this possibility. The chapter will wrap up with a few suggestions about angels and demons.

LIFE BEYOND LIFE: HOPE OR DESPAIR?

It is often thought that for there to be life after this life, there must be a soul—an immaterial self or person who is embodied and can survive the death of the physical body. It is often further thought that science has established that we are fully and only material bodies. I suggest that this is not the case. What the brain sciences have established is the correlation of the mental and the physical, but correlation is not identity. We have long known, from ancient Greco-Roman medicine to contemporary medicine, that our mental states—sensations, thoughts, and desires—are causally related to brain activity. We also have abundant reason to think that the mental and physical are not identical. If your mental life was the very same thing as your brain, then neuro-observation would equate to observing thoughts and mental states. In actuality, no study of the brain will amount to observing your thoughts, feelings, and sensations. What we have to do instead is infer what your mental life is on the basis of reports from you and other subjects and inferences to the best explanation of your behavior. This line of reasoning is called the *knowledge argument*. If A *is* B, whatever is true of A, is true of B. If water is H2O, then whatever is true of the one (I am drinking water right now) is true of the other (I am drinking H2O right now).[18] If the mind is the brain, to know the brain-events is to know the mental life, but this is not the case.

Many philosophers today are aware of the difficulty of identifying the mental and the physical. I cite a long passage from the work of a contemporary materialist, Michael Lockwood:

> Let me begin by nailing my colours to the mast. I count myself a materialist, in the sense that I take consciousness to be a species of brain activity. Having said that, however, it seems to me evident that no description of brain activity of the relevant kind, couched in the currently available languages of physics, physiology, or functional or computational roles, is remotely capable of capturing what is distinctive about consciousness. So glaring, indeed, are the shortcomings of all the reductive programmes currently on offer, that I cannot believe that anyone with a philosophical training, looking dispassionately at these programmes, would take any of them seriously for a moment, were it not for a deep-seated conviction that current physical science

18. See Taliaferro, "Substance Dualism: A Defence."

has essentially got reality taped, and accordingly, *something* along the lines of what the reductionists are offering *must* be correct. To that extent, the very existence of consciousness seems to me to be a standing demonstration of the explanatory limitations of contemporary physical science. On the assumption that some form of materialism is nevertheless true, we have only to introspect in order to recognize that our present understanding of matter is itself radically deficient. Consciousness remains for us, at the dawn of the twenty-first century, what it was for Newton at the dawn of the eighteenth century: an occult power that lies beyond the pool of illumination that physical theory casts on the world we inhabit.[19]

The current philosophical predicament has resulted from a failure to appreciate the birth of modern science. With Galileo and Newton, science was oriented to the study of mind-independent objects and their properties. Newton, for example, was concerned with the laws of motion involving inanimate objects. He was not concerned with the attraction and repulsion of human bodies based on romantic desire. Over time it has occurred to some philosophers that they know a great deal about the mind-independent physical, while the world of consciousness and the mental is mysterious. However, there would be no science at all without conscious, rational, mentally alert subjects. We only form an idea of a mind-independent reality by using and knowing our own minds. I join a number of philosophers (Like Noam Chomsky and Galen Strawson) who propose that we currently lack a problem-free concept of a mind-independent world. Keep in mind that all visual properties

19. Lockwood, *Consciousness*, 447.

and other sensibles (how things feel, taste, smell, sound) are all dependent on minds; they are mental properties.

There are abundant reasons other than the knowledge argument to think that there is more to us than our material bodies.[20] If these reasons carry the day, then there is room to believe that the destruction of the body does not entail the annihilation of the person. Even if materialism is true, some Christian philosophers have proposed that life after this life can occur either through resurrection or through God's re-creation of your body.[21]

Earlier in this chapter, I backed the view of Keith Ward and others that life after life is essential in the Christian view of the evils of this world. But imagine that the world did not contain horrific evil and that all persons lived until they were a hundred. Would death then be something evil or bad? Given our actual bodies and modern medicine, we might come to accept that a person can live a full life without desiring it to be extended. I suggest that this is where we should entertain the difference between our concept of being a person and our concept of being embodied or having the bodies we have. The biological life of our bodies has (as it were) a shelf-life. Our organs will run out. But it is a different matter when we think of what it is to be a person, a subject who loves, cares, plays, works, has relationships, including relations with other creatures and with God, and on and on. I suggest that the value of a person is inexhaustible such that a God who truly loves persons would not will that they cease to be.[22]

20. See Loose et al., eds., *Blackwell Companion to Substance Dualism*. I also defend what I call integrative dualism is my first book *Consciousness and the Mind of God*.

21. Current Christian materialists include Peter van Inwagen, Kevin Corcoran, and Trenton Merricks.

22. I argue for this in the article "Why We Need Immortality."

Furthermore, in the Christian tradition, humans were created by God *for* transformation into the likeness of God—that is our *telos*, our goal. The word often used to describe this holy transformation is *theosis*, our becoming like God, participating in the very life of God, through being united to God in Christ. Now, bringing a human to the destiny for which he or she was created—*theosis*—will require that death is not the end.

ANGELS AND DEMONS

None of the creeds of the Christian church call for us to believe that there are angels and demons, but angels and demons do play a role in the New Testament and in some Christian liturgy. If you share with me some skepticism about materialism, you may be open to recognizing that there may be intelligent, immaterial, good or evil agents. Actually, you might be open to there being angels and demons even on materialist philosophy, especially if you deny (as I do) the unity of space. I believe there are spatial objects that are not (as it were) in physical space. That is, I think there are spatial objects that are not spatially some distance from the spatial, material objects that surround us. So, I think that there are dream images and hallucinations (visual, spatial objects) that are not some distance from, say my desk. From a philosophical point of view, I do not know of any compelling reason to rule out there being angels and demons.

What role might angels and demons play in a Christian view of evil? I do not rule out the possibility of demonic possession, but I do suggest that appealing to the work of demons in accounting for evil acts is highly likely to be a means of avoiding taking responsibility for one's own acts. For this reason, I think most Christians today should doubt the role of the demonic in accounting for evil unless there is overwhelming evidence (perhaps from parapsychology) to the contrary. Belief in the work of angels, on the other hand, seems benign and may have a role in terms of edification.

An alternative approach to demonic powers is to think about talk of demons, spirits, and powers as a mythological way to speak about an important feature of human life in the world. There are economic, political, and social forces at work in the world beyond the individual choices of individual humans and those forces exert considerable influence on our lives. Of course, they have no existence apart from human social life, but they nevertheless have a reality that transcends any individual and they take on a life and potency of their own. These "powers" can be forces for good or evil. Think of crowd dynamics and the "spirit" of a crowd in similar terms—how people can be swept up into corrupt behavior by "principalities and powers" that we might speak of as "demonic." This raises the issue of social and structural evil, which transcends the choices of individuals.

Structural evil doesn't make the problem of evil any more intellectually difficult for faith in God, but it does have implications for how we confront evil and it does relate to the issue of redemptive narratives. According to Colossians 1:15–20, the invisible "powers" were created through Christ as a *good* aspect of creation. There is nothing inherently evil about them. However, they rebelled and "fell"—becoming demonic forces at work in the world. Yet the text goes on to speak of their "redemption" in Christ through his work on the cross. This suggests that the issue of redemption is more than the redemption of individuals but also of bigger "units." Maybe that is why Christian hope is new creation— a creationwide hope.

Overall, I suggest that the study of the ways in which demons and angels are portrayed in scripture, literature, and the arts can shed light on how to imagine evil and goodness. For example, Dante's depiction of Satan at the center of hell is a brilliant portrait of how evil can be self-defeating. Satan is stuck in a lake of ice; the more his wings move, the more frozen and trapped his condition. The portrait of angels as "flying babies" (to borrow a term from the art historian Margaret M. Miles) in paintings in the baroque era in Italy must have been a consoling image of life beyond this world, given the tragic number of children who died either at birth or at very young ages.

QUESTIONS FOR FURTHER DISCUSSION

1. Does the magnitude of evils demonstrate that God's existence is impossible, improbable, or neither?

2. Does an afterlife help in trying to make sense of suffering?

3. What evidence could there be that there is life after this life? Would ostensible out-of-the-body experiences, for instance, count as some evidence that persons can survive the death of their bodies?

4. Would a belief in life after this life enhance or compromise your sense of the meaning of this life?

5. When is the death of a person bad?

6. How do you interpret language about Satan or the devil? As a literal, non-physical intelligence, as a symbol for evil, or something else?

4

CONFRONTING EVIL WITH GOOD

PROVISIONAL DISTINCTIONS

"Do not be overcome by evil, but overcome evil with good," so St. Paul admonishes fellow Christians (Romans 12:21). Over the centuries, many Christian ethicists have wrestled with this precept. There is some appeal to adopting it in a strict, formal fashion, for if you endorse doing some evil to prevent a greater evil, you might find yourself on a slippery slope and have great difficulty getting off. If you think it your duty to kill three people in order to save four people, why might it not be a duty to kill 100 people to save 101 people? Not that all Christians using the Pauline principle are pacifists, but (as noted in chapter 1) most Christians believe that killing is a grave matter and should only be countenanced in extreme conditions.

It is the Pauline precept that encourages a focus on the good when challenging what is evil. The position defended earlier—evil is a deviation from or distortion of what is natural[1]—lends some support for the Pauline precept. We discover what is evil by noting how evil does not "get things right." Our goal should be to restore what is good by nature and to do so with our gaze upon what is good. This sometimes involves matters of intention. So, in a textbook illustration of the principle, imagine you and another person are starving to death. There is enough food for one of you to survive until there is a life-saving rescue. Most of us would think it a Christ-like act of self-sacrifice to give the food to the other person and perish as a result. However, Christians following the Pauline precept would find it problematic if the reason you gave the food to the other person is that you were seeking to commit suicide. (I should add quickly that contemporary Christians often have a nuanced view of suicide, realizing that it should not be treated as the equivalent of self-murder. Even so, we can imagine some cases, however rare, when it is like a self-murder.) The main point, though, is that the Pauline precept urges us to carry out our acts *with the intention of achieving a good*.

Let's consider four areas when evil is challenged from a Christian point of view.

---

1. A full account of evil as a deviation or distortion of what is natural will need to attend to an overall philosophy of the natural world itself. The lamb eaten by a lion suffers an ill or evil, but it is the outcome of the lion being a good lion. The overall goodness of an ecosystem in the natural world will inevitably involve a balance of the loss and generation of life. Holmes Rolston III and Robin Attfield have articulated Christian holistic accounts of the good of the natural world without losing sight of the goodness of the individuals (including predators and prey) that make it up.

THE PRIMACY OF SELF-EXAMINATION OVER JUDGING OTHERS

In Matthew 7:4–5, Jesus asks rhetorically "How can you say to your brother, 'Let me take the speck out of your eye,' while there is still a beam in your own eye? You hypocrite! First take the beam out of your own eye, and then you will see clearly to remove the speck from your brother's eye." It is interesting that Jesus is not precluding the judging of another person, but there is an unmistakable primacy given to judging or examining one's own character and action. Why? I suspect this has to do with how vanity or pride can bring us not to see our own faults. It may be because of pride that I shield my gaze from my own immersion in the seven deadly sins (vanity or pride, anger, lust, envy, sloth, avarice, and gluttony), I accuse someone else of being pompous, consumed with rage, being prurient, controlled by professional envy, lazy, greedy, and gluttonous.

Pride is commonly understood in Christian ethics as an inordinate desire for preeminence. It is also seen as a person's placing excessive importance on themselves in relationship to others. It is distinguishable from narcissism, however, as a narcissist may have excessive self-concern but despise themselves and regard themselves as less important than others. Most Christian ethicists have held that there is a proper pride that is healthy and co-extensive with humility. While humility involves a keen awareness of one's shortcomings and limitations, it is different from humiliation or false humility (e.g., a case of when an Olympic hockey player claims, falsely, that they are not very good at hockey).

Jesus's warning about distorted judgments of others goes hand in hand with Jesus's admonition:

> You have heard that it was said, "Love your neighbor and hate your enemy." 44 But I tell

you, love your enemies and pray for those who
persecute you, 45 that you may be children of
your Father in heaven. He causes his sun to
rise on the evil and the good, and sends rain
on the righteous and the unrighteous. 46 If you
love those who love you, what reward will you
get? Are not even the tax collectors doing that?
47 And if you greet only your own people, what
are you doing more than others? Do not even
pagans do that? 48 Be perfect, therefore, as your
heavenly Father is perfect.

(Matthew 5:43–48)

Rather than prudent reciprocation, Jesus appears to be
asking us to generously love others, especially those who
may have enmity against us. In light of such teachings, it
appears that when or if we critically assess others it must be
not only after we have purged ourselves of hierocracy, but
our assessment of others must also be loving.

THE PRIMACY OF LOVE OVER HATE

Would you rather have a police officer who hated injustice
or loved justice? The same question of a physician: would
you rather she went into medical practice because she loved
health or hated disease? Perhaps these are unfair questions,
but I raise them to note that when we are chiefly motivated
by that which we hate (and desire to eradicate injustice and
disease), our lives can be defined by that which we oppose
(and possibly loathe).

The twentieth-century philosopher Max Scheler
stressed the importance of Christians prizing the good in
his reply to Friedrich Nietzsche, the nineteenth-century
fierce critic of Christianity. In the *Genealogy of Morals* and
other books, Nietzsche proposed that the Christian teaching about the importance of humility and servanthood

was really based on a resentment of those who have power. Scheler conceded that there might be cases whence the critique of the powerful is based on resentment, but there are more cases in Christian tradition when what is prized (humility, charity) is because of its vital goodness, and not out of spite for what is condemned. In the vast majority of Christian accounts of redemption, it is held that redemption is offered by and through Christ for the sake of that which is good (Hebrews 12:2).

It is the primacy of love that underlies the Christian teaching about forgiveness and mercy, rather than an exclusive focus on justice as punishment. Compare the Christian notion on forgiveness (one should be ready to forgive multiple times, Matthew 18:21–35) with Heinrich Heine's famous, amusingly wicked view of forgiveness:

> Mine is a most peaceable disposition. My wishes are: a humble cottage with a thatched roof, but a good bed, good food, the freshest milk and butter, flowers before my window, and a few fine trees before my door; and if God wants to make my happiness complete, he will grant me the joy of seeing some six or seven of my enemies hanging from those trees. Before death I shall, moved in my heart, forgive them all the wrong they did me in their lifetime. One must, it is true, forgive one's enemies—but not before they have been hanged.[2]

Christian tradition has fostered a massive literature on the nature and power of love. There have been debates about the comparative value of personal, particular, loving relationships as distinct from the love that we owe to all persons. This was especially important (and still is today) in monastic communities. This was addressed brilliantly by

2. Heinrich Hein, cited in Freud, *Civilization and Its Discontents*.

the twelfth-century monastic St. Aelred of Rievaulx, who defended the value of special friendships as essential to our humanity. Debates have occurred on the difference between healthy love and obsession or lust; whether the love of neighbor should be utterly selfless or can be motivated by desire; whether marriage can be dissolved before death. From a Christian point of view, can you love another person too much?

Let us take up just the last question. For Christians, love is principally defined in terms of the good, both the good of the one loving and the one loved. This is sometimes abbreviated as the claim that love is beneficent. It has long been recognized that love also has a unitive dimension; the lover desires to be united with the beloved (in erotic love this may involve sexual intimacy, but in so-called Platonic love, this may be a desire to be in the company of the beloved). In the huge Christian literature on love, two important points stand out: loving another person presupposes some (healthy) self-love. The command to love your neighbor *as yourself* will not be effective if you do not love yourself. Second, beneficent love takes primacy over unitive love. That is, if it is neither good for you or for the beloved for there to be a unity of you both, then such a unity is not proper love, for it fails in terms of beneficence.

Assuming this philosophy of love, then there is reason to think you cannot love another person too much.

What of cases when someone seems to stay in a relationship because they love the person abusing them? Such cases would not be love, because (without exception) it is neither good for the person who thinks they are loving nor good for the abuser. What of a case of Romeo and Juliet when too much love led to a double suicide? Again, one reason for thinking this was a failure of love is that each "lover" carried out self-inflicted death, not a good for the other or for the relationship. I believe the same is true for other seeming cases of when a person seems to love another so much that they ruin each other's lives, and so on.

At the risk of being sued for over-generalizations, I make note of two other features of love from a Christian standpoint. The first is that Christianity has tended to give a special honor to unrequited love, cases of when someone loves another, and the love is not reciprocated. This is at the heart of Søren Kierkegaard's *Works of Love*. One of the reasons for this special honor is that Christians have stressed the primacy of loving *persons*, rather than (primarily) loving love. There is nothing wrong with loving love, but if you love the love of your partner/spouse/friend, and they cease to love you, the object of your love has ceased to be. Arguably, it is the stronger love (and person) who still longs for the good of the beloved (has beneficent love), even after she or he has ceased to return any love whatever.

A second point, Christians have differed on the extent that they see love as a feeling. There has been a tendency of some (such as Kierkegaard) to think of love primarily in terms of action. I address the unity of action and thought below, but here I stress that the majority of Christian philosophers and theologians have thought of love as suffused with desire, longing, and a desire to take joy in the beloved. Christian liturgy involving baptism, marriage, consecrations, and funerals would be utterly unintelligible if they were carried out by Stoics who sought to eradicate all emotions.

I end this section of the chapter with just one case of love involving great emotion. In *The Lord of the Rings*, J. R. R. Tolkien offers a Christian view of love as rooted in joy. Consider just one among many cases of laughter in the trilogy. In the third volume, when Gandalf is with the hobbit Pippin, just before the siege of Gondor, Pippin hears

Gandalf laugh. "Pippin glanced in some wonder at the face now close to his own, for the sound of that laugh had been gay and merry. Yet in the wizard's face he saw at first only lines of care and sorrow; though as he looked more intently he perceived that under all there was a great joy; a fountain of mirth enough to set a kingdom laughing, were it to gush forth."[3]

THE PRIMACY OF GLOBAL COMMUNITY OVER NATIONALISM AND INDIVIDUALISM

Karl Marx admired the portrait of the early Christians in Acts 4:32–35, according to which they held their property in common. Indeed, from the start of Christian monastic tradition in the third century, there has been a longstanding tradition of renouncing the accumulation of wealth and private property. Jesus tells his disciples to give to those in need (Matthew 5:2; Luke 6:30). Jesus also teaches that following him involves the transcending of family loyalties (Matthew 12:46–50).

While historically Christianity has had important links with imperial and national power, beginning with the fourth-century Roman Emperor Constantine the Great, there has always been a stress on how one's identity as a Christian and one's following Christ supersedes state authority and national identity (Acts 5:29). I am not suggesting that Christianity is incompatible with patriotism, but I suggest it is incompatible with a form of nationalism that denigrates others or that embodies vanity on a national level. The reason why many Christian leaders (Roman Catholic bishops, Episcopal and Anglican primates,

---

3. Tolkien, *The Return of the King*, 28. This image of Gandalf matches G. K. Chesterton's depiction of Christ at the end of his classic book *Orthodoxy*.

Protestant denominations like the Lutherans) oppose the immigration policies of the Donald Trump administration is on the grounds that it ignores those in need in the name of nationalism. The slogan "America First" seems to be the paradigm case of the classic Christian conception of vanity as the inordinate desire for preeminence.

From its beginning, Christianity was not defined by gender, national or imperial identity, or ethnicity: "There is neither Jew nor Gentile, neither slave nor free, nor is there male and female, for you are all one in Christ Jesus" (Galatians 3:28). Such a teaching encourages an international, cosmopolitan concern for the global community of persons.

THE PRIMACY OF THE DISPOSSESSED

The West has long had a tradition of praising worldly glory, power, and reputation. This can be seen in the earliest poem in the West, *The Iliad*. The portrait of aristocratic violence in that Homeric poem, as warriors seek to establish their glory (*kleos* in Greek) stands in dramatic contrast to the New Testament portrait of Christ among the dispossessed, those with diseases, prostitutes, others. One of Mother Teresa's favorite biblical verses was Matthew 25:40, 45: "Truly I tell you, whatever you did for one of the least of these brothers and sisters of mine, you did for me." From a Christian point of view, it is the vulnerable, the downtrodden, those who have been harmed that are vital.

In *A Black Theology of Liberation*, James Cone writes, "Any message that is not related to the liberation of the poor in a society is not Christ's message. Any theology that is indifferent to the terms of liberation is not Christian theology."[4]

---

4. Cited in Thorsen, *An Exploration of Christian Theology*, 31.

THE INDISSOLUBLE UNITY OF FAITH AND ACTION

One of the tests of one's religious faith is whether or not one truly acts on it. This is troubling because Christianity seems to demand a lot. Jesus tells us we are to give to the poor, to turn the other cheek, to give to the hungry, cloth the naked, visit those in prison.

In Shakespeare's *Hamlet*, we hear the line "words without thoughts, do not to heaven go." It might be added that neither thoughts nor words to heaven go unless they lead to concrete action. All we say or write about Christian faith will not be truly reflective of one's faith if there is no action behind it. Now, there could be a good reason why there is little action in some instances: physical disability, ill health, and social oppression, for example. But if there are occasions, it seems that living out one's faith in service to one another is essential.

I end with some personal reflections. One of the greatest fears I have is self-deception. I worry that when I profess to believe things, I may not deep down really and truly believe what I say. For example, I did not know (deep down) that I loved being a professor until I had the opportunity to not be a professor. When both my parents died some years ago, I inherited enough money so that I could meet all of my goals in writing and travel without a yearly salary as a professor. I came to a realization: I actually must truly love being a professor because I continue to be one even when not incentivized financially. I will retire from teaching at St. Olaf College in August of 2021, with the plan of teaching philosophy in prison for three years, starting in 2022. I will do so as a Christian philosopher who is concerned with prison reform and making life more oriented to rehabilitation. All sorts of reasons might prevent me from doing so (I might die of a heart attack tomorrow). But part of me wants to show both to myself and to others that I mean what I say when I claim to care about prison conditions, and I say what I mean. If you read this in 2022, feel free to check in with me and let me know of your own journey involving faith and philosophy.

To summarize this chapter, and indeed the heart of the entire book: the most important Christian response to evil is not an intellectual demonstration to explain why God allows evil, rather it is human lives lived in pursuit of the good and opposition to all that undermines it.

QUESTIONS FOR DISCUSSION

1. According to utilitarians, you should do that act which will produce the greatest happiness for the greatest number of people. While many Christian philosophers are not utilitarians, many early utilitarians were Anglican clergy. Should Christians be wary of utilitarianism?

2. The Pauline principle ("overcome evil with good") has not been upheld by all Christian theologians. Reinhold Niebuhr, for instance, adopted a form of realism, according to which sometimes one must do what is wrong to prevent greater wrongs. What is your view?

3. In Jesus's command to love our enemies, is Jesus commanding us to do something that is not natural?

SUGGESTIONS FOR FURTHER READING

Adams, Marilyn McCord. *Horrendous Evil and the Goodness of God*. Melbourne: Melbourne University Press, 1999.

Badham, Paul, and Linda Badham, eds. *Death and Immortality in the Religions of the World*. New York: Paragon House, 1987.

Hasker, William. *The Triumph of God over Evil*. Downers Grove, IL: IVP, 2008.

Meister, Chad. *Evil: A Guide for the Perplexed*. London: Bloomsbury, 2018.

Hick, John. *Death and Eternal Life*. Louisville, KY: Westminster/John Knox, 1994.

———. *Evil and the God of Love*. New York: HarperCollins, 1977.

Lewis, C. S. *The Problem of Pain*. New York: Macmillan, 1962.

Meister, Chad, and Paul Moser, eds. *The Cambridge Companion to the Problem of Evil*. Cambridge: Cambridge University Press, 2017.

Meister, Chad, and Charles Taliaferro. *The History of Evil*. 6 vols. London: Routledge, 2018.

Stump, Eleonore. *Wandering in Darkness*. Oxford: Oxford University Press, 2010.

Swinburne, Richard. *Providence and the Problem of Evil*. Oxford: Clarendon, 1998.

Taliaferro, Charles, and Jil Evans. *Is God Invisible? An Essay on Religion and Aesthetics*. Cambridge: Cambridge University Press, 2021.

BIBLIOGRAPHY

Abelard, Peter. "Exposition of the Epistle to the Romans." In *A Scholastic Miscellany: Anselm to Ockham*, edited by Eugene R. Fairweather, translated by Gerald E. Moffatt, 276–88. Philadelphia: Westminster, 1956.

Adams, Marilyn McCord. *Christ and Horrors: The Coherence of Christology*. Cambridge: Cambridge University Press, 2006.

———. "Horrendous Evils and the Goodness of God." In *The Problem of Evil*, edited by Marilyn Adams and Robert Merrihew Adams, 209–21. Oxford: Oxford University Press, 1990.

Alston, William. *Perceiving God: The Epistemology of Religious Experience*. Ithaca, NY: Cornell University Press, 1991.

Anscombe, G. E. M. *Intention*. 2nd ed. Ithaca, NY: Cornell University Press, 1963.

Anselm. *Anselm of Canterbury: The Major Works*. Edited by Brian Davies and G. R. Evans. Oxford: Oxford University Press, 1988.

———. "Why God Became Man." In *Anselm of Canterbury: The Major Works*, edited by Brian Davies and G. R. Evans, 260–356. Oxford: Oxford University Press, 1988.

Augustine. *The City of God*. Translated by Marcus Dods. Edinburgh: T. & T. Clark, 1871.

———. *Concerning the Nature of Good*. Edited by Philip Schaff, translated by John Newman. CreateSpace, 2015.

———. *On Christian Doctrine*. Translated by R. P. H. Green. Oxford: Clarendon, 1995.

Aulén, Gustaf. *Christus Victor*. Translated by H. G. Herbert. New York: MacMillan, 1969.

Boethius. *The Consolation of Philosophy*. Translated by D. R. Taylor. Cambridge: Harvard University Press, 1973.

Bibliography

Boswell, John. *Christianity, Tolerance and Homosexuality*. Chicago: University of Chicago Press, 1981.

Bourke, Vernon. *The Essential Augustine*. Indianapolis: Hackett, 1974.

Carson, Tomas. *Lying: Theory and Practice*. Oxford: Oxford University Press, 2010.

Clement, Olivier. *The Roots of Christian Mysticism*. New York: New City Pres, 1993.

Cohn-Sherbok, Dan. "Jewish Faith and the Holocaust." *Religious Studies* 26.2 (1990) 277–93.

Collins, Robin. "The Fine Tuning of the Cosmos Is Convincing" In *Debating Christian Theism*, edited by J. P. Moreland et al., 35–46. Oxford: Oxford University Press, 2013.

Copan, Paul. *Did God Really Command Genocide?* Grand Rapids: Baker, 2014.

———. *Is God a Moral Monster? Making Sense of the Old Testament God*. Grand Rapids: Baker, 2011

Cross, Richard. *The Metaphysics of the Incarnation: Thomas Aquinas to Duns Scotus*. Oxford: Oxford University Press, 2002.

Davis, Caroline F. *The Evidential Force of Religious Experience*. Oxford: Clarendon, 1989.

Davis, Stephen. "The Gospels Are Reliable as Historically Factual Accounts." In *Debating Christian Theism*, edited by J. P. Moreland et al., 417–29. Oxford: Oxford University Press, 2013.

Dawkins, Richard. *River Out of Eden: A Darwinian Way of Life*. New York: Basic, 1993.

Earman, John. *Hume's Abject Failure: The Argument against Miracles*. Oxford: Oxford University Press, 2000.

Evans, C. Stephen. *Natural Signs and the Knowledge of God*. Oxford: Oxford University Press, 2010.

Forrest, B. K., and A. E. McGrath, eds. *The History of Apologetics: A Biographical and Methodological Introduction*. Grand Rapids: Zondervan, 2020.

Freud, Sigmund. *Civilization and Its Discontents*. Translated by James Strachey. London: Penguin, 2002.

Gavrilyuk, Paul, and Sarah Coakley, eds. *The Spiritual Senses: Perceiving God in Western Christianity*. Cambridge: Cambridge University Press, 2011.

Gellman, Jerome. *Experience of God and the Rationality of Religious Belief*. Ithaca, NY: Cornell University Press, 1997.

———. *Mystical Experience of God*. Aldershot, UK: Ashgate, 2001.

Griffith, Paul. *Decreation: The Last Things of All Creatures*. Waco, TX: Baylor University Press, 2014.

———. *Lying: An Augustinian Theology of Duplicity*. Grand Rapids: Brazos, 2004.

Gutting, Gary. *Religious Belief and Religious Skepticism*. Notre Dame, IN: University of Notre Dame Press, 1982.

———. *What Philosophy Can Do*. New York: Norton, 2015.

Hart, David Bentley. *That All Shall Be Saved: Heaven, Hell, and Universal Salvation*. New Haven: Yale University Press, 2019.

Harvey, S. A. *Sensing Salvation: Ancient Christianity and the Olfactory Imagination*. Berkeley: University of California Press, 2006.

Hay, David. *Religious Experience Today: Studying the Facts*. London: Bloomsbury, 1990.

Hick, John. *Evil and the God of Love*. San Francisco: Harper and Row, 1978.

———. *The Fifth Dimension: An Exploration of the Spiritual Realm*. Oxford: Oneworld, 2004.

———. *A John Hick Reader*. Edited by Paul Badham. New York: Springer, 1990.

———. *Philosophy of Religion*. Upper Saddle River, NY: Prentice Hall, 1963.

Kwan, Kai-man. *The Rainbow of Experiences, Critical Trust, and God*. London: Continuum, 2011.

Keener, Craig. *The Credibility of the New Testament*. Grand Rapids: Baker, 2011.

———. *Miracles: The Credibility of the New Testament Accounts*. 2 vols. Grand Rapids: Baker, 2011.

Kierkegaard, Søren. *Fear and Trembling*. Edited by C. Stephen Evans and Sylvia Walsh. Cambridge: Cambridge University Press, 2006.

———. *Provocations*. Walden, NY: Plough, 2014.

Langland, William. *Piers the Ploughman*. Translated by J. F. Goodridge. Harmondsworth, UK: Penguin, 1974.

Lazare, Aaron. *On Apology*. Oxford: Oxford University Press, 2004.

Lockwood, Michael. *Consciousness: New Philosophical Perspectives*. Edited by Quentin Smith and Aleksandar Jokic. Oxford: Oxford University Press, 2003.

Loose, Jonathan, et al., eds. *Blackwell Companion to Substance Dualism*. Oxford: Wiley-Blackwell, 2018.

MacDonald, Gregory. *The Evangelical Universalist*. 2nd ed. Eugene, OR: Cascade, 2012.

Moore, Gareth. *A Question of Truth: Christianity and Homosexuality*. London: Continuum, 2003.

Moreland, J. P., et al., eds. *Debating Christian Theism*. Oxford: Oxford University Press, 2013.

Bibliography

Moorhead, John. "Boethius." In *The History of Evil in the Medieval Age: 450–1450* CE, edited by Andrew Pinsent, 23–35. London: Routledge, 2018.

Morris, Thomas. *The Logic of God Incarnate.* Ithaca, NY: Cornell University Press, 1986.

Murray, Michael. *Nature Red Tooth and Claw: Theism and the Problem of Animal Suffering.* Oxford: Oxford University Press, 2008.

Newberg, Andrew, and Mark Waldman. *How God Changes Your Brain: Breakthrough Findings from a Leading Neuroscientist.* New York: Ballantine, 2009.

Oderberg, David. *The Metaphysics of Good and Evil.* London: Routledge, 2020.

Pinsent, Andrew. "Aquinas." In *The History of Evil in the Medieval Age: 450–1450* CE, edited by Andrew Pinsent, 157–212. London: Routledge, 2018.

Plantinga, Alvin. *The Nature of Necessity.* Oxford: Oxford University Press, 1974.

———. "Self-Profile." In *Alvin Plantinga,* edited by James E. Tomberlin and Peter van Inwagen, 3–97. Dordrecht: Reidel, 1985.

Plato. *Euthyphro.* Translated by G. M. A. Grube. In *Plato: Complete Works,* edited by John Cooper, 1–16. Indianapolis: Hackett Publishing Company, 1997.

Reitan, Eric, and John Kronen. *God's Final Victory: A Comparative Philosophical Case for Universalism.* New York: Continuum, 2011.

Rice, Richard. *The Future of Open Theism: From Antecedents to Opportunities.* Downers Grove, IL: IVP, 2020.

Rogers, Katherine. *Perfect Being Theology.* Edinburgh: University of Edinburgh Press, 2000.

Rolston, Holmes. *Genes, Genesis, and God.* Cambridge: Cambridge University Press, 1999.

Scruton, Roger. *Sexual Desire: A Philosophical Investigation.* London: Continuum, 2006.

Soelle, Dorothee. *The Strength of the Weak: Towards a Christian Feminist Identity.* Philadelphia: Westminster, 1984.

Stump, Eleonore. *Atonement.* Oxford: Oxford University Press, 2018.

———. *Wandering in Darkness: Narrative and the Problem of Suffering.* Oxford: Oxford University Press, 2010.

Stump, J. B., and Chad Meister, eds. *Original Sin and the Fall: Five Views.* Downers Grove, IL: IVP Academic, 2020.

Swinburne, Richard. *The Christian God.* Oxford: Oxford University Press, 1994.

———. *The Coherence of Theism.* Rev. ed. Oxford: Clarendon, 1993.

———. *The Existence of God.* Oxford: Clarendon, 1979.

———. *Providence and the Problem of Evil.* Oxford: Oxford University, 1998.

———. *Responsibility and Atonement.* Oxford: Oxford University Press, 1989.

———. *The Resurrection of the Son of God.* Oxford: Oxford University Press, 2003.

Sykes, S. W., ed. *Sacrifice and Redemption: Durham Essays in Theology.* Cambridge: Cambridge University Press, 1991.

Talbott, Thomas. *The Inescapable Love of God.* 2nd ed. Eugene, OR: Cascade, 2014.

Taliaferro, Charles. *Consciousness and the Mind of God.* Cambridge: Cambridge University Press, 1994.

———. "In Defence of the Numinous." In *Philosophy and the Christian Worldview,* edited by D. Werther and M. Linville, 95–108. London: Continuum, 2012.

———. *Evidence and Faith: Philosophy and Religion since the Seventeenth Century.* Cambridge: Cambridge University Press, 2005.

———. *The Golden Cord: A Short Book on the Secular and the Sacred.* Notre Dame, IN: University of Notre Dame Press, 2012.

———, ed. *History of Evil, Vol. 1. Evil in Antiquity.* London: Routledge, 2018.

———, ed. *History of Evil, Vol. 2. Evil in the Middle Ages.* London: Routledge, 2018.

———, ed. *History of Evil, Vol. 3. Evil in the Early Modern Age.* London: Routledge, 2018.

———, ed. *History of Evil, Vol. 4. Evil in the 18th and 19th Centuries.* London: Routledge, 2018.

———, ed. *History of Evil, Vol. 5. Evil in the Early 20th Century.* London: Routledge, 2018.

———, ed. *History of Evil, Vol. 6. Evil from the Mid-20th Century to Today.* London: Routledge, 2018.

———. "The Jealousy of God." *New Oxford Review,* Jan-Feb, 1990, 12–15.

———. *Love. Love. Love: Light Reflections on Love, Life, and Death.* Cambridge: Cowley, 2010.

———. "Substance Dualism: A Defence." In *The Blackwell Companion to Substance Dualism,* edited by J. Loose et al., 43–59. Oxford: Wiley Blackwell, 2018.

———. "The Vanity of God." *Faith and Philosophy* 6.2 (1989) 140–54.

————. "Why We Need Immortality." *Modern Theology* 6.4 (1990) 367–79.

Taliaferro, Charles, and Jil Evans, eds. *Turning Images in Philosophy, Science, and Religion.* Oxford: Oxford University Press, 2011.

————. *Is God Invisible? An Essay on Religion and Aesthetic.* Cambridge: Cambridge University Press, 2021.

Taliaferro, Charles, and Chad Meister. *Contemporary Philosophical Theology.* London: Routledge, 2016.

Taliaferro, Charles, and Alison Tepley, eds. *Cambridge Platonist Spirituality.* Mahwah, NJ: Paulist, 2005.

Tenenbaum, Sergio. *Appearance of the Good.* Cambridge: Cambridge University Press, 2007.

Theresa of Avila. *The Life of Teresa of Jesus: The Autobiography of St. Teresa of Avila.* Translated by Allison Peers. Garden City, NY: Doubleday, 1960.

Thorson, Don. *An Exploration of Christian Theology.* 2nd ed. Grand Rapids: Baker, 2020.

Tolkien, J. R. R. *The Return of the King.* London: The Folio Society, 1977.

Twelftree, Graham, ed. *The Cambridge Companion to Miracles.* Cambridge: Cambridge University Press, 2011.

Underhill, Evelyn. *Mysticism.* 1910. Reprint, Oxford: Oneworld, 1999.

van Inwagen, Peter. "The Place of Chance in a World Sustained by God." In *Divine and Human Action*, edited by Thomas V. Morris, 211–35. Ithaca, NY: Cornell University Press, 1988.

Wainwright, William. *Mysticism.* Madison, WI: University of Wisconsin Press, 1981.

Walls, Jerry. *Hell: The Logic of Damnation.* Notre Dame, IN: University of Notre Dame Press, 1992.

————, ed. *The Oxford Handbook of Eschatology.* Oxford: Oxford University Press, 2010.

————. *Purgatory: The Logic of Total Transformation.* Oxford: Oxford University Press, 2011.

Ward, Keith. *The Big Questions in Science and Religion.* West Conshohocken, PA: Templeton, 2008.

————. *God: A Guide for the Perplexed.* Oxford: Oneworld, 2002.

————. *Is Religion Dangerous?* Grand Rapids: Eerdmans, 2007.

————. *Rational Theology and the Creativity of God.* Oxford: Blackwell, 1982.

Wright, N. T. *The Resurrection of the Son of God.* London: SPCK, 2003.

Yandell, Keith. *The Epistemology of Religious Experience.* Cambridge: Cambridge University Press, 1999.